TO

FROM

FRIENDS

100 Days to Figure THEM Out!

TEEN SERIES devos 100

The quoted ideas expressed in this book (but not Scripture verses) are not, in all cases, exact quotations, as some have been edited for clarity and brevity. In all cases, the author has attempted to maintain the speaker's original intent. In some cases, quoted material for this book was obtained from secondary sources, primarily print media. While every effort was made to ensure the accuracy of these sources, the accuracy cannot be guaranteed. For additions, deletions, corrections, or clarifications in future editions of this text, please write Freeman-Smith, LLC.

Scripture quotations are taken from:

The Holy Bible, King James Version

The Holy Bible, New International Version (NIV) Copyright © 1973, 1978, 1984, by International Bible Society. Used by permission of Zondervan Publishing House. All rights reserved.

The New American Standard Bible®, (NASB) Copyright © 1960, 1962, 1963, 1968, 1971, 1972, 1973, 1975, 1977, 1995 by The Lockman Foundation. Used by permission.

The Holy Bible, New King James Version (NKJV) Copyright © 1982 by Thomas Nelson, Inc. Used by permission.

The Holy Bible, New Living Translation, (NLT) Copyright © 1996. Used by permission of Tyndale House Publishers, Inc., Wheaton, Illinois 60189. All rights reserved.

New Century Version®, (NCV) Copyright © 1987, 1988, 1991 by Word Publishing, a division of Thomas Nelson, Inc. All rights reserved. Used by permission.

The Message (MSG) This edition issued by contractual arrangement with NavPress, a division of The Navigators, U.S.A. Originally published by NavPress in English as THE MESSAGE: The Bible in Contemporary Language copyright 2002-2003 by Eugene Peterson. All rights reserved.

The Holman Christian Standard Bible™ (HOLMAN CSB) Copyright © 1999, 2000, 2001 by Holman Bible Publishers. Used by permission.

Cover Design by Kim Russell / Wahoo Designs
Page Layout by Bart Dawson

ISBN 978-1-60587-099-1

Printed in the United States of America

FRIENDS

100 Days to Figure THEM Out!

TEEN SERIES | devos

Introduction

S ometimes friends can be hard to figure out—hard, but not impossible. With God's help and a little practice, you can understand your friends, you can choose the right friends, and you can be a better friend.

Throughout the Bible, we are reminded to love one another, to care for one another, and to treat one another as we wish to be treated. In other words, we are reminded to be good Christians, and we are reminded to be good friends.

This text contains 100 devotional readings. The ideas in each chapter are powerful reminders of God's commandments—and of the importance of choosing friends who encourage you to be obedient and faithful. So here's your assignment: Today and every day, resolve to be a trustworthy, encouraging, loyal friend. And, while you're at it, treasure the people in your life who are loyal friends to you. Friendship is, after all, a glorious gift, praised by God. Give thanks for that gift and make it grow.

Pleasing God First

You shall have no other gods before Me.

Exodus 20:3 NKJV

Here's a quick quiz: Whose expectations are you trying to meet? A. Your friends' expectations, B. Society's expectations, C. God's expectations.

If you're a Christian, the correct answer is C., but if you're overly concerned with either A. or B., you're not alone. Plenty of people invest too much energy trying to please their peers' expectations and too little energy trying to please God. It's a common behavior, but it's also a very big mistake.

A better strategy, of course, is to try to please God first. To do so, you must prioritize your life—and your relationships—according to God's commandments.

Are you having trouble choosing between God's priorities and society's priorities? Are you feeling overwhelmed by peer pressure? Are you feeling pressured or confused? If so, turn the concerns over to God—prayerfully, earnestly, and often. Then, listen for His answer . . . and trust the answer He gives.

One with God is a majority.

When all else is gone, God is left,
and nothing changes Him.

God doesn't want shares of your life;
He wants controlling interest!

Figuring Out Friendships: Place God first in every aspect of your life, including your friendships. He deserves first place, and any relationship that doesn't put Him there is the wrong relationship for you.

Choosing Friends Carefully

As iron sharpens iron, a friend sharpens a friend.
Proverbs 27:17 NLT

Some friendships help us honor God; these friendships should be nurtured. Other friendships place us in situations where we are tempted to dishonor God by disobeying His commandments; friendships that dishonor God have the potential to do us great harm.

Because we tend to become like our friends, we must choose our friends carefully. Because our friends influence us in ways that are both subtle and powerful, we must ensure that our friendships are pleasing to God. When we spend our days in the presence of godly believers, we are blessed, not only by those friends, but also by our Creator.

Do you seek to live a life that is pleasing to God? If so, you should build friendships that are pleasing to Him. When you do, your Heavenly Father will bless you and your friends with gifts that are simply too numerous to count.

You could have been born in another time
and another place, but God determined to "people"
your life with these particular friends.

Joni Eareckson Tada

Don't bypass the potential for meaningful friendships
just because of differences.
Explore them. Embrace them. Love them.

Luci Swindoll

The glory of friendship is not the outstretched hand,
or the kindly smile, or the joy of companionship.
It is the spiritual inspiration that comes to one when he
discovers that someone else believes in him
and is willing to trust him with his friendship.

Corrie ten Boom

Figuring Out Friendships: Your friends will be a
major influence on your life. So please choose your
friends very, very carefully.

Find Friends Who Help You Make Wise Choices

I am offering you life or death, blessings or curses.
Now, choose life! . . . To choose life is to love
the Lord your God, obey him, and stay close to him.

Deuteronomy 30:19-20 NCV

Face facts: your life is a series of choices. From the instant you wake up in the morning until the moment you nod off to sleep at night, you make countless decisions—decisions about the things you do, decisions about the words you speak, and decisions about the way that you choose to direct your thoughts.

As a believer who has been transformed by the amazing love of Jesus, you have every reason to make wise choices. But sometimes, when the daily grind threatens to grind you up and spit you out, you may make choices that are displeasing to God. When you do, you'll pay a price because you'll forfeit the happiness and the peace that might otherwise have been yours.

So, as you pause to consider the kind of Christian you are—and the kind of friends you want to associate with—

ask yourself whether you're sitting on the fence or standing in the light. And while you're at it, ask yourself whether you're choosing friends who help you make smart choices, not dumb ones. Remember: if you sincerely want to follow in the footsteps of the One from Galilee, you must make choices that are pleasing to Him. He deserves no less . . . and neither, for that matter, do you.

Choices can change our lives profoundly.
The choice to mend a broken relationship, to say "yes" to a difficult assignment, to lay aside some important work to play with a child, to visit some forgotten person—these small choices may affect many lives eternally.

Gloria Gaither

Figuring Out Friendships: Remember that the friends you choose can make a profound impact on every other aspect of your life. So choose carefully and prayerfully.

Too Much Stuff?

He who trusts in his riches will fall,
but the righteous will flourish . . . .
Proverbs 11:28 NKJV

Are your friends overly concerned with the stuff that money can buy? Hopefully not. On the grand stage of a well-lived life, material possessions should play a rather small role. Of course, we all need the basic necessities of life, but once we meet those needs for ourselves and for our families, the piling up of possessions creates more problems than it solves. Our real riches, of course, are not of this world. We are never really rich until we are rich in spirit.

Our society is in love with money and the things that money can buy. God is not. God cares about people, not possessions, and so must we. We must, to the best of our abilities, love our neighbors as ourselves, and we must, to the best of our abilities, resist the mighty temptation to place possessions ahead of people.

Money, in and of itself, is not evil; worshipping money is. So today, as you prioritize matters of importance in your life, remember that God is almighty, but the dollar is not.

Greed is enslaving. The more you have,
the more you want—
until eventually avarice consumes you.

Kay Arthur

As faithful stewards of what we have,
ought we not to give earnest thought
to our staggering surplus?

Elisabeth Elliot

Here's a simple test: If you can see it, it's not going to last.
The things that last are the things you cannot see.

Dennis Swanberg

Remember This: Material possessions aren't
really that important—and hopefully material
possessions aren't too important to you and your
friends.

Don't Try to Please People, Try to Please God

Do you think I am trying to make people accept me?
No, God is the One I am trying to please.
Am I trying to please people? If I still wanted to please
people, I would not be a servant of Christ.

Galatians 1:10 NCV

Sometimes, it's very tempting to be a people-pleaser. But usually, it's the wrong thing to do.

When you worry too much about pleasing your friends, you may not worry enough about pleasing God—and when you fail to please God, you inevitably pay a very high price for your mistaken priorities.

Whom will you try to please today: God or your friends? Your obligation is most certainly not to your peers. Your obligation is to an all-knowing and perfect God. Trust Him always. Love Him always. Praise Him always. And seek to please Him and only Him. Always.

When we are set free from the bondage of pleasing others, when we are free from currying others' favor and others' approval—then no one will be able to make us miserable or dissatisfied. And then, if we know we have pleased God, contentment will be our consolation.

Kay Arthur

Every day, I find countless opportunities to decide whether I will obey God and demonstrate my love for Him or try to please myself or the world system. God is waiting for my choices.

Bill Bright

Figuring Out Friendships: If you are burdened with a "people-pleasing" personality, outgrow it. Realize that you can't please all of the people all of the time (including all of your friends), nor should you attempt to.

First, Focus on the Spiritual Stuff

For those whose lives are according to the flesh think about the things of the flesh, but those whose lives are according to the Spirit, about the things of the Spirit.

Romans 8:5 Holman CSB

Is Christ the focus of your life? Are you fired with enthusiasm for Him? Are you an energized Christian who allows God's Son to reign over every aspect of your day? Make no mistake: that's exactly what God intends for you to do.

God has given you the gift of eternal life through His Son. In response to God's priceless gift, you are instructed to focus your thoughts, your prayers, and your energies upon God and His only begotten Son. To do so, you must resist the subtle yet powerful temptation to become a "spiritual dabbler."

A person who dabbles in the Christian faith is unwilling to place God in His rightful place: above all other things. Resist that temptation; make God the cornerstone and the touchstone of your life—including your friendships. When you do, He will give you all the strength and wisdom you need to live victoriously for Him.

Whatever we focus on determines what we become.

E. Stanley Jones

Blessed are those who know what on earth they are here on earth to do and set themselves about the business of doing it.

Max Lucado

If the glories of heaven were more real to us, if we lived less for material things and more for things eternal and spiritual, we would be less easily disturbed in this present life.

Billy Graham

Remember This: First, you should focus on God . . . and then everything else will come into focus.

Make Friends at Church

God is Spirit, and those who worship Him
must worship in spirit and truth.

John 4:24 Holman CSB

A great place to find friends—and keep them—is in a local church.

Are you an active, contributing, member of your local fellowship? The answer to this simple question will have a profound impact on the quality and direction of your spiritual journey.

So, if you are not currently engaged in a local church, do yourself a favor: Find a church that you're comfortable with, and join it. And once you've joined, don't just attend church out of habit. Go to church out of a sincere desire to know and worship God. When you do, you'll be blessed by the men and women who attend your fellowship, and you'll be blessed by your Creator. You deserve to attend church, and God deserves for you to attend church, so don't delay.

Christians are like coals of a fire.
Together they glow—apart they grow cold.

Anonymous

And if our fellowship below in Jesus be so sweet,
what greater blessings shall we know when
'round His throne we meet?

Charles Wesley

One of the ways God refills us after failure is through
the blessing of Christian fellowship. Just experiencing
the joy of simple activities shared with other children
of God can have a healing effect on us.

Anne Graham Lotz

Remember This: Here is a short list of things God
wants you and your friends to do:
1. Go to church.
2. Pay attention in church.
3. Support the church.
4. Enjoy the fellowship of the people you meet in
church. End of sermon.

Remember: Cooperation Builds Relationships

Work at getting along with each other and with God. Otherwise you'll never get so much as a glimpse of God.

Hebrews 12:14 MSG

D o your friends understand the importance of cooperation? Or are you hanging out with people who are just a little more self-centered than that? And before you answer, here's something to consider: good friends learn the wisdom of "give and take," not the foolishness of "me first."

Cooperative relationships flourish over time—one-sided relationships don't. So if you're trying to become friends with someone who says, "It's my way or the highway," choose the highway. And choose it now.

Before God changes our circumstances,
He wants to change our hearts.

Warren Wiersbe

Teamwork makes the dream work.

John Maxwell

Cooperation is a two-way street,
but for too many couples,
it's the road less traveled.

Marie T. Freeman

Figuring Out Friendships: Cooperation pays. When you cooperate with your friends, you'll feel good about yourself—and your friends will feel good about you, too.

Find Friends Who Encourage You to Hope

Rejoice in hope; be patient in affliction;
be persistent in prayer.

Romans 12:12 Holman CSB

Face facts: pessimism and Christianity don't mix. Why? Because Christians have every reason to be optimistic about life here on earth and life eternal. Mrs. Charles E. Cowman advised, "Never yield to gloomy anticipation. Place your hope and confidence in God. He has no record of failure."

Sometimes, despite our trust in God, we may fall into the spiritual traps of worry, frustration, anxiety, or sheer exhaustion, and our hearts become heavy. What's needed is plenty of rest, a large dose of perspective, and God's healing touch, but not necessarily in that order.

Today, make this promise to yourself and keep it: vow to be a hope-filled Christian. And while you're at it, find friends who help you think optimistically about your life, your education, and your future. Trust your hopes, not your fears. Take time to celebrate God's glorious creation. And then, when you've filled your heart with hope, share your optimism with others. They'll be better for it, and so will you. But not necessarily in that order.

The people whom I have seen succeed best in life
have always been cheerful and hopeful people who went
about their business with a smile on their faces.

Charles Kingsley

It is a remarkable thing that some of the most optimistic
and enthusiastic people you will meet are those
who have been through intense suffering.

Warren Wiersbe

Developing a positive attitude means working continually
to find what is uplifting and encouraging.

Barbara Johnson

Figuring Out Friendships: Optimistic friends will help you become a more optimistic person.

Use God's Word as the Guide

All Scripture is inspired by God and is profitable for teaching,
for rebuking, for correcting, for training in righteousness,
so that the man of God may be complete,
equipped for every good work.

2 Timothy 3:16-17 Holman CSB

If you'd like to know what God has to say about your friendships, here's how you can find out. Read the book He wrote—it's called the Bible and it has timeless advice for life here on earth and life eternal.

The Bible is unlike any other book. It is a priceless gift from your Creator, a tool that God intends for you to use in every aspect of your life. And, it contains promises upon which you, as a Christian, can and must depend.

God's Word can be a roadmap to successful relationships and spiritual abundance. Make it your roadmap. God's wisdom can be a light to guide your steps. Claim it as your light today, tomorrow, and every day of your life—and then walk confidently in the footsteps of God's only begotten Son.

You may as well quit reading and hearing
the Word of God, and give it to the devil,
if you do not desire to live according to it.

Martin Luther

God can see clearly no matter how dark or
foggy the night is.
Trust His Word to guide you safely home.

Lisa Whelchel

It takes calm, thoughtful, prayerful meditation
on the Word to extract its deepest nourishment.

Vance Havner

Remember This: You can make Bible study a team
sport. When two people study the Word together,
God blesses them and their friendship.

Listen Carefully to Your Conscience

Let us come near to God with a sincere heart and a sure faith,
because we have been made free from a guilty conscience,
and our bodies have been washed with pure water.

Hebrews 10:22 NCV

I f you and your friends are about to do something that you know is wrong, a little voice inside your head has a way of speaking up. That voice, of course, is your conscience: an early-warning system designed to keep you out of trouble. If you listen to that voice, you'll be okay; if you ignore it, you're asking for headaches, or heartbreaks, or both.

Few things in life will torment you more than a guilty conscience. Thankfully, the reverse is also true: a clear conscience is a lasting reward that becomes yours when you know that you've done the right thing.

Whenever you're about to make an important decision, you should listen carefully to the quiet voice inside. Sometimes, of course, it's tempting to do otherwise. From time to time you'll be tempted to abandon your better judgment by ignoring your conscience. But remember: a conscience is a terrible thing to waste. So instead of ignoring that quiet little voice, pay careful attention to it. If you do, your conscience will lead you in the right direction—in fact, it's trying to lead you right now. So listen . . . and learn.

To go against one's conscience is neither safe nor right. Here I stand. I cannot do otherwise.

Martin Luther

The convicting work of the Holy Spirit awakens, disturbs, and judges.

Franklin Graham

A good conscience is a continual feast.

Francis Bacon

Remember This: The more important the decision . . . the more carefully you should listen to your conscience.

Don't Be Too Critical

Do not judge, and you will not be judged.
Do not condemn, and you will not be condemned.
Forgive, and you will be forgiven.

Luke 6:37 Holman CSB

From experience, we know that it is easier to criticize than to correct; we understand that it is easier to find faults than solutions; and we realize that excessive criticism is usually destructive, not productive. Yet the urge to criticize others remains a powerful temptation for most of us. Our task, as obedient believers, is to break the twin habits of negative thinking and critical speech.

Negativity is highly contagious: we give it to our friends who, in turn, give it back to us. This cycle can be broken by positive thoughts, heartfelt prayers, and encouraging words. As thoughtful servants of a loving God, we can use the transforming power of Christ's love to break the chains of negativity. And we should.

When something robs you of your peace of mind, ask
yourself if it is worth the energy you are expending on it.
If not, then put it out of your mind in an act of discipline.
Every time the thought of "it" returns, refuse it.

Kay Arthur

Discouraged people, if they must be discouraged, ought,
at least, to keep their discouragements to themselves,
hidden away in the privacy of their own bosoms lest they
should discourage the hearts of their brethren.

Hannah Whitall Smith

Being critical of others, including God, is one way
we try to avoid facing and judging our own sins.

Warren Wiersbe

Figuring Out Friendships: If you're tempted to be
critical of others, remember that your ability to
judge others requires a level of insight that you
simply don't have. So do everybody (including
yourself) a favor: don't criticize.

Trust God's Plans

You will teach me how to live a holy life.
Being with you will fill me with joy;
at your right hand I will find pleasure forever.

Psalm 16:11 NCV

The Bible makes it clear: God's got a plan—a very big plan—and you're an important part of that plan. But here's the catch: God won't force His plans upon you; you've got to figure things out for yourself . . . or not.

As a follower of Christ, you should ask yourself this question: "How closely can I make my plans match God's plans?" The more closely you manage to follow the path that God intends for your life, the better.

Do you have questions or concerns about your friendships? Take them to God in prayer. Do you have hopes and expectations? Talk to God about your dreams. Are you carefully planning for the days and weeks ahead? Consult God as you establish your priorities. Turn every concern over to your Heavenly Father, and sincerely seek His guidance—prayerfully, earnestly, and often. Then, listen for His answers . . . and trust the answers that He gives.

God possesses infinite knowledge and awareness which is uniquely His. At all times, even in the midst of any type of suffering, I can realize that He knows, loves, watches, understands, and more than that, He has a purpose.

Billy Graham

I don't doubt that the Holy Spirit guides your decisions from within when you make them with the intention of pleasing God. The error would be to think that He speaks only within, whereas in reality He speaks also through Scripture, the Church, Christian friends, and books.

C. S. Lewis

The God who orchestrates the universe has a good many things to consider that have not occurred to me, and it is well that I leave them to Him.

Elisabeth Elliot

Figuring Out Friendships: When life seems unfair, try spending more time trusting God and less time dwelling on "the unfairness of it all."

Be Forewarned: Dishonesty and Immorality Eat Away at Your Heart, Your Soul, and Your Friendships

*The righteousness of the blameless clears his path,
but the wicked person will fall because of his wickedness.*

Proverbs 11:5 Holman CSB

When you become involved in friendships that require you to compromise your values, you'll make yourself miserable. Why? Because God has given you a conscience that tells you right from wrong, that's why.

It has been said that character is what you are when nobody is watching. How true. But, as Bill Hybels correctly observed, "Every secret act of character, conviction, and courage has been observed in living color by our omniscient God." And isn't that a sobering thought?

If you sincerely wish to walk with God, you must seek, to the best of your ability, to follow His commandments. When you do, your character will take care of itself . . . and you won't need to look over your shoulder to see who, besides God, is watching.

The single most important element
in any human relationship is honesty—
with oneself, with God, and with others.

Catherine Marshall

The great test of a man's character is his tongue.

Oswald Chambers

Figuring Out Friendships: Never accept blatant dishonesty as a part of any friendship, and never accept physical or emotional abuse from anyone, especially those people who are closest to you.

Don't Make Impulsive Decisions That Might Affect the Rest of Your Life

*Happy is the person who finds wisdom,
the one who gets understanding.*

Proverbs 3:13 NCV

Are you and your friends, at times, just a little bit impulsive? Do you occasionally leap before you look? Do you react first and think about your reaction second? If so, God wants to have a little chat with you.

God's Word is clear: as believers, we are called to lead lives of discipline, diligence, moderation, and maturity. But the world often tempts us to behave otherwise. Everywhere we turn, or so it seems, we are faced with powerful temptations to behave in undisciplined, ungodly ways.

God's Word instructs us to be disciplined in our thoughts and our actions; God's Word warns us against the dangers of impulsive behavior. God's Word teaches us that "anger" is only one letter away from "danger." And, as believers in a just God who means what He says, we should act—and react—accordingly.

Very few things motivate us to give God our undivided attention like being faced with the negative consequences of our decisions.

Charles Stanley

Wisdom is the right use of knowledge.
To know is not to be wise. Many men know a great deal, and are all the greater fools for it.
But to know how to use knowledge is to have wisdom.

C. H. Spurgeon

The fruit of wisdom is Christlikeness, peace, humility, and love. And, the root of it is faith in Christ as the manifested wisdom of God.

J. I. Packer

Remember This: Put the brakes on impulsive behavior . . . before impulsive behavior puts the brakes on you.

Be a Disciple

Therefore, be imitators of God, as dearly loved children.

Ephesians 5:1 Holman CSB

Whom will you walk with today? Will you and your friends walk with people who worship the ways of the world? Or will you walk with the Son of God?

Jesus walks with you. Are you walking with Him? Hopefully, you will choose to walk with Him today and every day of your life.

Jesus has called upon believers of every generation (and that includes you) to follow in His footsteps. And God's Word promises that when you follow in Christ's footsteps, you will learn how to live freely and lightly (Matthew 11:28-30).

Are you worried about the day ahead? Be confident in God's power. He will never desert you. Are you concerned about the future? Be courageous and call upon God. He will protect you. Are you confused? Listen to the quiet voice of your Heavenly Father. He is not a God of confusion. Talk with God; listen to Him; follow His commandments . . . and walk with His Son—starting now.

Discipleship usually brings us into the necessity
of choice between duty and desire.

Elisabeth Elliot

Be filled with the Holy Spirit; join a church where
the members believe the Bible and know the Lord;
seek the fellowship of other Christians;
learn and be nourished by God's Word and His many
promises. Conversion is not the end of your journey—
it is only the beginning.

Corrie ten Boom

We cannot make disciples of others
unless we are disciples ourselves.

Oswald Chambers

Figuring Out Friendships: It's up to you to follow
Christ, and one good way to do it is to find friends
who will follow Him with you.

Find Friends Who Don't Expect You to Be Perfect

Those who wait for perfect weather will never plant seeds;
those who look at every cloud will never harvest crops.
Plant early in the morning, and work until evening,
because you don't know if this or that will succeed.
They might both do well.

Ecclesiastes 11:4,6 NCV

You and your friends live in a world where expectations are high, incredibly high, or unreachable. The media delivers an endless stream of messages that tell you how to look, how to behave, how to eat, and how to dress. The media's expectations are impossible to meet—God's are not. God doesn't expect you to be perfect . . . and neither should you.

If you find yourself bound up by the chains of perfectionism, it's time to ask yourself who you're trying to impress, and why. If you're trying to impress other people, it's time to reconsider your priorities.

Remember this: the expectations that really matter are not society's expectations or your friends' expectations.

The expectations that matter are God's expectations, pure and simple. And everything else should take a back seat.

So do your best to please God, and don't worry too much about what other people think. And, when it comes to meeting the unrealistic expectations of our crazy world, forget about trying to meet those unrealistic expectations and concentrate, instead, on living a life that's pleasing to God.

God is so inconceivably good. He's not looking for perfection. He already saw it in Christ.
He's looking for affection.

Beth Moore

The happiest people in the world are not those who have no problems, but the people who have learned to live with those things that are less than perfect.

James Dobson

Remember This: You don't have to be perfect to be wonderful.

Don't Be Afraid to Ask God for Help

You do not have because you do not ask.

James 4:2 Holman CSB

I f you want to know more about your friendships, ask God for His help! When you ask sincerely—and repeatedly—He will answer your request.

How often do you ask God for His guidance and His wisdom? Occasionally? Intermittently? Whenever you experience a crisis? Hopefully not. Hopefully, you've acquired the habit of asking for God's assistance early and often. And hopefully, you have learned to seek His guidance in every aspect of your life.

We get into trouble when we think we know what to do and we stop asking God if we're doing it.

Stormie Omartian

Notice that we must ask. And we will sometimes struggle to hear and struggle with what we hear. But personally, it's worth it. I'm after the path of life— and he alone knows it.

John Eldredge

When you ask God to do something, don't ask timidly; put your whole heart into it.

Marie T. Freeman

Figuring Out Friendships: If you want more from your life or your friendships, ask for God's help— and keep asking—until He answers your prayers.

Find Friends Who Forgive

*Be even-tempered, content with second place,
quick to forgive an offense. Forgive as quickly and completely
as the Master forgave you. And regardless of what else you
put on, wear love. It's your basic, all-purpose garment.
Never be without it.*

Colossians 3:13-14 MSG

A re you and your friends the kind of people who have a tough time forgiving and forgetting? If so, welcome to the club. Most of us find it difficult to forgive the people who have hurt us. And that's too bad because life would be much simpler if we could forgive people "once and for all" and be done with it. Yet forgiveness is seldom that easy. Usually, the decision to forgive is straightforward, but the process of forgiving is more difficult. Forgiveness is a journey that requires effort, time, perseverance, and prayer.

If there exists even one person whom you have not forgiven (and that includes yourself), obey God's commandment: forgive that person today. And remember that bitterness, anger, and regret are not part of God's plan for your life. Forgiveness is.

If you sincerely wish to forgive someone, pray for that person. And then pray for yourself by asking God to heal your heart. Don't expect forgiveness to be easy or quick, but rest assured: with God as your partner, you can forgive . . . and you will.

When God forgives, He forgets. He buries our sins
in the sea and puts a sign on the shore saying,
"No Fishing Allowed."
Corrie ten Boom

God expects us to forgive others as He has forgiven us;
we are to follow His example
by having a forgiving heart.
Vonette Bright

To hold on to hate and resentments is to throw
a monkey wrench into the machinery of life.
E. Stanley Jones

Remember This: It's simple: friends forgive friends.

Keep Your Priorities in Line with God's Priorities

Come near to God, and God will come near to you.
You sinners, clean sin out of your lives.
You who are trying to follow God and the world
at the same time, make your thinking pure.

James 4:8 NCV

Have you fervently asked God to help prioritize your life? Have you asked Him for guidance and for the courage to do the things that you know need to be done? If so, then you're continually inviting your Creator to reveal Himself in a variety of ways. As a follower of Christ, you must do no less.

When you make God's priorities your priorities, you will receive God's abundance and His peace. When you make God a full partner in every aspect of your life, He will lead you along the proper path: His path. When you allow God to reign over your heart, He will honor you with spiritual blessings that are simply too numerous to count. So, as you build your relationships and live your life, make God's will your ultimate priority. When you do, every other priority will have a tendency to fall neatly into place.

A disciple is a follower of Christ. That means you take on His priorities as your own. His agenda becomes your agenda. His mission becomes your mission.

Charles Stanley

Have you prayed about your resources lately? Find out how God wants you to use your time and your money. No matter what it costs, forsake all that is not of God.

Kay Arthur

Sin is largely a matter of mistaken priorities. Any sin in us that is cherished, hidden, and not confessed will cut the nerve center of our faith.

Catherine Marshall

Remember This: Your Heavenly Father wants you to prioritize your day and your life. And the best place to start is by putting God first.

Find the Right Crowd

Don't become partners with those who reject God. How can you make a partnership out of right and wrong? That's not partnership; that's war. Is light best friends with dark?

2 Corinthians 6:14 MSG

If you hang out with people who do dumb things, pretty soon, you'll probably find yourself doing dumb things, too. And that's bad . . . very bad. So here's an ironclad rule for earning more self-respect and more rewards from life: If your peer group is headed in the wrong direction, find another peer group, and fast. Otherwise, before you know it, you'll be caught up in trouble that you didn't create and you don't deserve.

Peer pressure can be good or bad, depending upon who your peers are and how they behave. If your friends encourage you to follow God's will and to obey His commandments, then you'll experience positive peer pressure, and that's a good thing. But, if your friends encourage you to do foolish things, then you're facing a different kind of peer pressure . . . and you'd better beware.

When you feel pressured to do things—or to say things—that lead you away from God, you're heading straight for trouble. So don't do the "easy" thing or the "popular" thing. Do the right thing, and don't worry about winning any popularity contests.

> It is comfortable to know that we are responsible to God and not to man. It is a small matter to be judged of man's judgement.
>
> Lottie Moon

> I have found that the closer I am to the godly people around me, the easier it is for me to live a righteous life because they hold me accountable.
>
> John MacArthur

Figuring Out Friendships: Put peer pressure to work for you: How? By associating with people who, by their actions and their words, will encourage you to become a better person.

Treat Mind-altering Substances Like Poison
(Because That's What They Are!)

Be sober! Be on the alert!
Your adversary the Devil is prowling around like a
roaring lion, looking for anyone he can devour.

I Peter 5:8 Holman CSB

D
o you hang out with people who consider "party-ing" to be the most important aspect of their lives? If so, you're headed headlong down a dead-end street . . . right along with your friends.

Mind-altering substances (including the most popular American mind-bender of all: good old-fashioned beer) are dangerous . . . make that Dangerous (with a capital D).

So here are three things to remember about alcohol and other drugs:

1. If you're drinking or drugging, you must either stop that behavior or face very disastrous consequences.

2. If you're spending time with people who think that alcohol and drugs are "harmless," you're choosing to associate with some very naïve people.

3. If you're dating someone who drinks or drugs, you deserve better . . . much better. End of lecture.

> To many, total abstinence is easier than perfect moderation.
>
> St. Augustine

> Addiction is the most powerful psychic enemy of humanity's desire for God.
>
> Gerald May

> Whatever you love most, be it sports, pleasure, business or God, that is your god.
>
> Billy Graham

Remember This: Make Jesus your highest priority, and ask Him to help you overcome any behaviors that might distance you from Him.

Find Friends Who Help You Obey God

Those who obey his commands live in him, and he in them.
And this is how we know that he lives in us:
We know it by the Spirit he gave us.

1 John 3:24 NIV

D o you look for friends who can help you become a better Christian? Hopefully so, because obedience to Him is rewarded and disobedience isn't.

Since God created Adam and Eve, we human beings have been rebelling against our Creator. Why? Because we are unwilling to trust God's Word, and we are unwilling to follow His commandments. God has given us a guidebook for righteous living called the Holy Bible. It contains thorough instructions which, if followed, lead to fulfillment, righteousness, and salvation. But, if we choose to ignore God's commandments, the results are as predictable as they are tragic.

Unless we are willing to abide by God's laws, all of our righteous proclamations ring hollow. How can we best proclaim our love for the Lord? By obeying Him. And, for further instructions, read the manual.

We are always making an offering.
If we do not give to God, we give to the devil.

Vance Havner

God's love for His children is unconditional, no strings
attached. But, God's blessings on our lives do come with
a condition—obedience. If we are to receive
the fullness of God's blessings, we must obey Him and
keep His commandments.

Jim Gallery

It takes faith to obey God,
but God always rewards obedient faith.

Warren Wiersbe

Remember This: Obedience leads to spiritual
growth: Anne Graham Lotz correctly observed,
"If you want to discover your spiritual gifts, start
obeying God. As you serve Him, you will find that
He has given you the gifts that are necessary to
follow through in obedience."

Build Relationships That Will Last

And regardless of what else you put on, wear love. It's your basic, all-purpose garment. Never be without it. Let the peace of Christ keep you in tune with each other, in step with each other. None of this going off and doing your own thing. And cultivate thankfulness.

Colossians 3:14-15 MSG

D o you want to build friendships that last? Then you must start by making God the cornerstone of your friendships.

God does not intend for you to experience mediocre relationships; He created you for far greater things. Building lasting relationships requires compassion, wisdom, empathy, kindness, courtesy, and forgiveness (lots of forgiveness). If that sounds a lot like work, it is—which is perfectly fine with God. Why? Because He knows that you are capable of doing that work, and because He knows that the fruits of your labors will enrich the lives of you and your friends, now and for many years to come.

Living life with a consistent spiritual walk deeply
influences those we love most.

Vonette Bright

Healthy relationships include laughter.
Every relationship, whether it is with your spouse
or your children, can be filled with joy and with laughter.

Dennis Swanberg

Line by line, moment by moment, special times are etched
into our memories in the permanent ink of everlasting
love in our relationships.

Gloria Gaither

Figuring Out Friendships: Communication is vital
to the health on any friendship. If you're having
trouble expressing yourself, don't clam up. Instead,
keep trying until you finally get the hang of it.

Insist upon Shared Values

Be on guard. Stand true to what you believe.
Be courageous. Be strong.
I Corinthians 16:13 NLT

Whether you realize it or not, your character is shaped by your values. From the time your alarm clock wakes you in the morning until the moment you lay your head on the pillow at night, your actions are guided by the values that you hold most dear. If you're a thoughtful believer, then those values are shaped by the Word of God.

Society seeks to impose its set of values upon you and your friends, but these values are often contrary to God's Word (and thus contrary to your own best interests). The world makes promises that it simply cannot fulfill. It promises happiness, contentment, prosperity, and abundance. But genuine abundance is not a byproduct of possessions or status; it is a byproduct of your thoughts, your actions, and your relationship with God. The world's promises are incomplete and deceptive; God's promises are unfailing. Your challenge, then, is to build your value system upon the firm foundation of God's promises . . . nothing else will suffice.

As a citizen of the 21st century, you live in a world that is filled with countless opportunities to make big-time mistakes. The world seems to cry, "Worship me with your time, your money, your energy, and your thoughts!" But God commands otherwise: He commands you to worship Him and Him alone; everything else must be secondary.

Do you want to strengthen your character? If so, then you must build your life upon a value system that puts God first. So, when you're faced with a difficult choice or a powerful temptation, seek God's counsel and trust the counsel that He gives. Invite God into your heart and live according to His commandments. Study His Word and talk to Him often. When you do, you will share in the abundance and peace that only God can give.

As the first community to which a person is attached
and the first authority under which a person learns to live,
the family established society's most basic values.

Charles Colson

Figuring Out Friendships: When making judgments about friends and dates, don't focus on appearances, focus on values.

Don't Overestimate the Importance of Appearances

As the water reflects the face, so the heart reflects the person.

Proverbs 27:19 Holman CSB

The world sees you as you appear to be; God sees you as you really are. He sees your heart, and He understands your intentions. The opinions of others should be relatively unimportant to you; however, God's view of you—His understanding of your actions, your thoughts, and your motivations—should be vitally important.

Few things in life are more futile than "keeping up appearances" in order to impress your friends—yet the media would have you believe otherwise. The media would have you believe that everything depends on the color of your hair, the condition of your wardrobe, and the model of the car you drive. But nothing could be further from the truth. What is important, of course, is pleasing your Father in heaven. You please Him when your intentions are pure and your actions are just. When you do, you will be blessed today, tomorrow, and forever.

Pride opens the door to every other sin, for once we are more concerned with our reputation than our character, there is no end to the things we will do just to make ourselves "look good" before others.

Warren Wiersbe

If the narrative of the Scriptures teaches us anything, from the serpent in the Garden to the carpenter in Nazareth, it teaches us that things are rarely what they seem, that we shouldn't be fooled by appearances.

John Eldredge

Remember This: Judging other people solely by appearances is tempting, but it's foolish, shortsighted, immature, and ultimately destructive. So don't do it.

Pray About It!

If you don't know what you're doing, pray to the Father.
He loves to help. You'll get his help, and won't be
condescended to when you ask for it. Ask boldly, believingly,
without a second thought. People who "worry their prayers"
are like wind-whipped waves. Don't think you're
going to get anything from the Master that way,
adrift at sea, keeping all your options open.

James 1:5-8 MSG

Andrew Murray observed, "Some people pray just to pray, and some people pray to know God." Your task, as a maturing believer, is to pray, not out of habit or obligation, but out of a sincere desire to know your Heavenly Father. Through constant prayers, you should petition God, you should praise Him, and you should seek to discover His unfolding plans for your life.

Today, reach out to the Giver of all blessings. Turn to Him for guidance and for strength. Invite Him into every corner of your day. When you have questions about friendships, or anything else for that matter, ask God to teach you and to lead you. And remember that no matter your circumstances, God is here . . . always right here. So pray.

Prayer succeeds when all else fails.

E. M. Bounds

Where there is much prayer, there will be much
of the Spirit; where there is much of the Spirit,
there will be ever-increasing power.

Andrew Murray

He who is his own guide is guided by a fool.

C. H. Spurgeon

Remember This: Prayer changes things, it changes
you, and it changes other people. So pray.

Learn How to Deal with Rejection

*I've told you all this so that trusting me,
you will be unshakable and assured, deeply at peace.
In this godless world you will continue to experience
difficulties. But take heart! I've conquered the world.*

John 16:33 MSG

Sometimes, you may feel pressured to compromise yourself, and you may be afraid of what will happen if you firmly say no to your friends. You may be afraid that you'll be rejected. But here's a tip: don't worry too much about rejection, especially when you're rejected for doing the right thing.

Pleasing other people is a good thing . . . up to a point. But you must never allow your "willingness to please" to interfere with your own good judgement or with God's commandments.

Instead of being afraid of rejection, focus on pleasing your Creator first and always. And when it comes to the world and all its inhabitants, don't worry too much about the folks you can't please. Focus, instead, on doing the right thing—and leave the rest up to God.

You must never sacrifice your relationship with God for the sake of a relationship with another person.

Charles Stanley

A healthy self-identity is seeing yourself as God sees you—no more and no less.

Josh McDowell

Confidence in the natural world is self-reliance; in the spiritual world, it is God-reliance.

Oswald Chambers

Figuring Out Friendships: If you have a choice between pleasing people and pleasing God . . . please God!

Insist upon Mutual Respect

Here is a simple, rule-of-thumb for behavior:
Ask yourself what you want people to do for you, then grab
the initiative and do it for them. Add up God's Law and
Prophets and this is what you get.

Matthew 7:12 MSG

D o you respect yourself enough to demand that your friends respect you, too? Please, please, please answer that question with a resounding YES! Why? Because if you don't respect yourself, other people may find it easy to take advantage of you.

Think about it like this: the more you respect yourself, the more likely you are to make smart decisions . . . and the smarter decisions you make, the more reasons you'll have to respect yourself—it's a cycle of good decision making that reinforces a well-deserved, positive self-image.

But what if you find that your self-image could use a tune-up? Well, try these five simple steps: 1. Don't do things that you know to be immoral, imprudent, or impulsive. 2. Make the conscious effort to invest yourself in activities that improve your own life and the lives of others. 3. If you're beset by negative self-talk, put an immediate stop to the mindless ramblings of your inner critic. 4. Associate yourself with people who encourage you to think and behave in ways that are pleasing to God. 5. Ask your Heavenly Father to guide your path and direct your thoughts.

When you take these simple steps, you'll respect yourself more, and you'll demand the same kind of respect from others.

> You are valuable just because you exist.
> Not because of what you do or what you have done,
> but simply because you are.
>
> Max Lucado

Remember This: If you're currently doing things that betray your principles or your conscience, stop it. And if you're having a hard time accepting yourself, ask yourself this question: "If God loves me, then why shouldn't I love myself?"

Remember That Real Worship Requires Obedience

God is spirit, and those who worship him
must worship in spirit and truth.

John 4:24 NCV

All of mankind is engaged in the practice of worship. Some people choose to worship God and, as a result, reap the joy that He intends for His children. Others distance themselves from God by worshiping such things as earthly possessions or personal gratification. …and when they do, they suffer.

What will you choose to worship today? Will you and your friends worship your Creator or your possessions? Will you worship your Savior, Jesus Christ, or will you bow down before the false gods of pride and popularity? Will you seek the approval of your God or the approval of your peers? Every day provides opportunities to put God where He belongs: at the center of your life. Worship Him—and only Him—today, tomorrow, and always.

True faith commits us to obedience.

A. W. Tozer

Disobedience to His Word will cause you to doubt.

Anne Graham Lotz

Our obedience does not make God any bigger or better than He already is. Anything God commands of us is so that our joy may be full—the joy of seeing His glory revealed to us and in us!

Beth Moore

Remember This: God rewards obedience and punishes disobedience. It's not enough to understand God's rules; you must also live by them . . . or else.

Find Friends Who Make Smart Choices

He that walketh with wise men shall be wise:
but a companion of fools shall be destroyed.

Proverbs 13:20 KJV

Some friends encourage you to obey God—these friends help you make wise choices. Other friends put you in situations where you are tempted to disobey God—these friends tempt you to make unwise choices.

Are you hanging out with—and dating—people who, by their presence and their influence, make you a better Christian? Or are you spending time with people who encourage you to stray from your faith? The answer to this question will help determine the condition of both your relationships and your spiritual health. One of the best ways to ensure that you follow Christ is to find fellow believers who are willing to follow Him with you. And if you can't find friends like that, you're looking in the wrong places.

You will get untold flak for prioritizing God's revealed
and present will for your life over man's . . .
but, boy, is it worth it.

Beth Moore

We, as God's people, are not only to stay far away
from sin and sinners who would entice us,
but we are to be so like our God that we mourn over sin.

Kay Arthur

Those who follow the crowd usually get lost in it.

Rick Warren

Figuring Out Friendships: If you want to meet new
people, go to the places where you are likely to
bump into the kind of people you want to meet:
you probably won't find the right kind of person in
the wrong kind of place.

Beware of Temptations

No temptation has overtaken you except
what is common to humanity. God is faithful and
He will not allow you to be tempted beyond what you are
able, but with the temptation He will also provide
a way of escape, so that you are able to bear it.

1 Corinthians 10:13 Holman CSB

You've got to admit that you and your friends live in a temptation-filled world. The devil is hard at work in your neighborhood, and so are his helpers. Here in the 21st century, the bad guys are working around the clock to lead you astray. That's why you must remain vigilant.

In a letter to believers, Peter offers a stern warning: "Your adversary, the devil, prowls around like a roaring lion, seeking someone to devour" (1 Peter 5:8 NASB). What was true in New Testament times is equally true in our own. Satan tempts his prey and then devours them (and it's up to you—and only you—to make sure that you're not one of the ones being devoured!).

As a young adult in search of godly relationships, you must beware because temptations are everywhere. Satan is determined to win; you must be equally determined that he does not.

Our Lord has given us an example of how to overcome
the devil's temptations. When He was tempted
in the wilderness, He defeated Satan every time
by the use of the Bible.

Billy Graham

Take a really honest look at yourself. Have any old sins
begun to take control again? This would be
a wonderful time to allow Him to bring fresh order
out of longstanding chaos.

Charles Swindoll

Remember This: If life's inevitable temptations seem to be getting the best of you, try praying more often, even if many of those prayers are simply brief, "open-eyed" requests to your Father in heaven.

Be Hungry for Righteousness

Blessed are those who hunger and thirst for righteousness,
because they will be filled.

Matthew 5:6 Holman CSB

Do you want to be a righteous person, and do you want to experience righteous relationships? Are you bound and determined—despite the inevitable temptations and distractions of our modern age—to be an example of godly behavior to your family and your friends? If so, you must "hunger and thirst" for righteousness. What, precisely, do the words "hunger and thirst" mean? Simply this: you must yearn to be righteous; you must strive to be righteous; and you must work to be righteous by putting aside many of the things that the world holds dear.

You will not become righteous by accident. You must hunger for righteousness, and when you do, you will be filled.

Have your heart right with Christ, and he will visit you often, and so turn weekdays into Sundays, meals into sacraments, homes into temples, and earth into heaven.

C. H. Spurgeon

Impurity is not just a wrong action; impurity is the state of mind and heart and soul which is just the opposite of purity and wholeness.

A. W. Tozer

Our souls were made to live in an upper atmosphere, and we stifle and choke if we live on any lower level. Our eyes were made to look off from these heavenly heights, and our vision is distorted by any lower gazing.

Hannah Whitall Smith

Figuring Out Friendships: The world's value system is flawed. God's value system is not. Search for friends who value God's system more and the world's system less.

Find Friends Who Encourage You to Be a Disciplined Person

But I discipline my body and bring it into subjection,
lest, when I have preached to others,
I myself should become disqualified.

I Corinthians 9:27 NKJV

Are you a self-disciplined person? And do your friends encourage you to be disciplined? If so, congratulations . . . your disciplined approach to life can help you build a more meaningful relationship with God. Why? Because God expects all His believers (including you) to lead lives of disciplined obedience to Him . . . and He rewards those believers who do.

God doesn't reward laziness, misbehavior, or apathy. God is less concerned with your party time than He is with your prayer time. And God wants all His followers (including you) to behave with dignity and self-control.

Sometimes, it's hard to be dignified and disciplined. Why? Because you live in a world where many prominent people want you to believe that dignified, self-disciplined behavior is going out of style. But don't kid yourself: self-discipline never goes out of style.

Face facts: Life's greatest rewards aren't likely to fall into your lap. To the contrary, your greatest accomplishments will probably require plenty of work and a heaping helping of self-discipline—which, by the way, is perfectly fine with God. After all, He knows that you're up to the task, and He has big plans for you. God will do His part to fulfill those plans, and the rest, of course, depends upon you.

The alternative to discipline is disaster.

Vance Havner

Personal humility is a spiritual discipline
and the hallmark of the service of Jesus.

Franklin Graham

Figuring Out Friendships: If you choose disciplined friends, you're more likely to become a more disciplined person.

Look for Fulfillment in All the Right Places

I am the Gate. Anyone who goes through me will be cared for—will freely go in and out, and find pasture. A thief is only there to steal and kill and destroy. I came so they can have real and eternal life, more and better life than they ever dreamed of. I am the Good Shepherd. The Good Shepherd puts the sheep before himself, sacrifices himself if necessary.

John 10:9-11 MSG

Where can you and your friends find fulfillment? Is it a result of money, or popularity, or looks, or material possessions? Hardly. Genuine contentment is a gift from God to those who trust Him and follow His commandments.

Our world seems preoccupied with the search for happiness. We are bombarded with messages telling us that happiness depends upon the acquisition of more and more stuff. These messages are false.

If we don't find contentment in God, we will never find it anywhere else. But, if we seek Him and obey Him, we will be blessed with an inner peace that is beyond human understanding. When God dwells at the center of our lives, peace and contentment will belong to us just as surely as we belong to God.

We will never be happy until we make God the source of our fulfillment and the answer to our longings.

Stormie Omartian

We're prone to want God to change our circumstances, but He wants to change our character.
We think that peace comes from the outside in, but it comes from the inside out.

Warren Wiersbe

By trying to grab fulfillment everywhere, we find it nowhere.

Elisabeth Elliot

Figuring Out Friendships: First, focus on your friendship with Jesus. Then, you'll find that other friendships will be more fulfilling.

Be a Good Example

For am I now trying to win the favor of people, or God?
Or am I striving to please people? If I were still trying to
please people, I would not be a slave of Christ.

Galatians 1:10 Holman CSB

How do your friends know that you're a Christian?
Well, you can tell them, of course. And make no
mistake about it: talking about your faith in God
is a very good thing to do. But simply telling people about
Jesus isn't enough. You must also be willing to show people
how an extremely devoted Christian (like you) should behave.

Is your life a picture book of your creed? Do your actions line up with your beliefs? Are you willing to practice
the philosophy that you preach? If so, congratulations. If
not, it's time for a change.

Like it or not, your behavior is a powerful example to
others. The question is not whether you will be an example
to your family and friends; the question is what kind of example will you be.

Corrie ten Boom advised, "Don't worry about what you
do not understand. Worry about what you do understand

in the Bible but do not live by." And that's sound advice because your family and friends are always watching . . . and so, for that matter, is God.

Too many Christians have geared their program to please, to entertain, and to gain favor from this world. We are concerned with how much, instead of how little, like this age we can become.

Billy Graham

Nothing speaks louder or more powerfully than a life of integrity.

Charles Swindoll

In your desire to share the gospel, you may be the only Jesus someone else will ever meet. Be real and be involved with people.

Barbara Johnson

Figuring Out Friendships: You and your friends set examples for each other. So you should set the right kind of example for your friends . . . and vice-versa.

Find Friends Who Help You Celebrate Life

Celebrate God all day, every day. I mean, revel in him!

Philippians 4:4 MSG

What is the best day for you and your friends to celebrate life? This one! Today and every day should be a time for celebration as you consider God's blessings (starting, of course, with God's ultimate gift: salvation through Jesus Christ).

What do you and your pals expect from the day ahead? Are you expecting God to do wonderful things, or are you living beneath a cloud of worry and doubt?

The familiar words of Psalm 118:24 remind us of a profound yet simple truth: "This is the day the Lord has made; let us rejoice and be glad in it" (Holman CSB). Our duty, as believers, is to rejoice in God's marvelous creation.

For Christians, every day begins and ends with God and His Son. Christ came to this earth to give us abundant life and eternal salvation. We give thanks to our Maker when we treasure each day. So with no further ado, let the celebration begin!

If you can forgive the person you were, accept the person you are, and believe in the person you will become, you are headed for joy. So celebrate your life.

Barbara Johnson

Joy is the direct result of having God's perspective on our daily lives and the effect of loving our Lord enough to obey His commands and trust His promises.

Bill Bright

Our sense of joy, satisfaction, and fulfillment in life increases, no matter what the circumstances, if we are in the center of God's will.

Billy Graham

Remember This: Your life should be a cause for celebration, and your friends should help you celebrate.

Trust God's Promises

Patient endurance is what you need now,
so you will continue to do God's will.
Then you will receive all that he has promised.

Hebrews 10:36 NLT

Want to improve your life and your relationships? Try paying a little more attention to God's promises. God has made quite a few promises to you, and He intends to keep every single one of them. You will find these promises in a book like no other: the Holy Bible. The Bible is your roadmap for life here on earth and for life eternal—as a believer, you are called upon to trust its promises, to follow its commandments, and to share its Good News.

God's promises never fail and they never grow old. You must trust those promises and share them with your friends, with your family, and with the world . . . starting now . . . and ending never.

There are four words I wish we would never forget,
and they are, "God keeps His word."

Charles Swindoll

The promises of Scripture are not mere pious hopes or
sanctified guesses. They are more than sentimental words
to be printed on decorated cards for Sunday School
children. They are eternal verities. They are true.
There is no perhaps about them.

Peter Marshall

We honor God by asking for great things when they
are a part of His promise. We dishonor Him and cheat
ourselves when we ask for molehills where He has
promised mountains.

Vance Havner

Remember This: Today is a great day to trust God's
promises. When you do, you will worry less and
enjoy life more.

Share Your Testimony

This and this only has been my appointed work:
getting this news to those who have never heard of God,
and explaining how it works by
simple faith and plain truth.

1 Timothy 2:7 MSG

A good way to build your faith is by talking about it—to friends, to family members, and even to strangers—and that's precisely what God wants you to do.

It's no secret: You live in a world that desperately needs the healing message of Jesus Christ. Every believer, including you, bears responsibility for sharing the Good News. And it is important to remember that you give your testimony through your words and your actions.

So today, preach the Gospel through your words and your deeds…but not necessarily in that order.

Your light is the truth of the Gospel message itself
as well as your witness as to Who Jesus is and what
He has done for you. Don't hide it.

Anne Graham Lotz

There is nothing anybody else can do that can stop God
from using us. We can turn everything into a testimony.

Corrie ten Boom

There is nothing more appealing or convincing
to a watching world than to hear the testimony of
someone who has just been with Jesus.

Henry Blackaby

Remember This: Whether you realize it or not,
you have a profound responsibility to tell as many
friends as you can about the eternal life that Christ
offers to those who believe in Him.

Live on Purpose

God chose you to be his people,
so I urge you now to live the life
to which God called you.

Ephesians 4:1 NCV

L ife is best lived on purpose. And purpose, like everything else in the universe, begins with God. Whether you realize it or not, God has a plan for your life and for your friendships. It's a divine calling, a direction in which He is leading you. When you welcome God into your heart and establish a genuine relationship with Him, He will begin, in time, to make His purposes known.

Sometimes, God's intentions will be clear to you; other times, God's plan will seem uncertain at best. But even on those difficult days when you are unsure which way to turn, you must never lose sight of these overriding facts: God created you for a reason; He has important work for you to do; and He's waiting patiently for you to do it.

And the next step is up to you.

The born-again Christian sees life not as a blurred, confused, meaningless mass, but as something planned and purposeful.

Billy Graham

It is important to set goals because if you do not have a plan, a goal, a direction, a purpose, and a focus, you are not going to accomplish anything for the glory of God.

Bill Bright

Only God's chosen task for you will ultimately satisfy. Do not wait until it is too late to realize the privilege of serving Him in His chosen position for you.

Beth Moore

Remember This: Discovering God's purpose for your life requires a willingness to be open. God's plan is unfolding day by day. If you keep your eyes and your heart open, He'll reveal His plans. God has big things in store for you, but He may have quite a few lessons to teach you before you are fully prepared to do His will and fulfill His purposes.

Don't Be Trapped by Envy

We can't afford to waste a minute, must not squander these precious daylight hours in frivolity and indulgence, in sleeping around and dissipation, in bickering and grabbing everything in sight. Get out of bed and get dressed! Don't loiter and linger, waiting until the very last minute. Dress yourselves in Christ, and be up and about!

Romans 13:13-14 MSG

Because we are frail, imperfect human beings, we are sometimes envious of others. But God's Word warns us that envy is sin. Thus, we must guard ourselves against the natural tendency to feel resentment and jealousy when other people experience good fortune.

As believers, we have absolutely no reason to be envious of any people on earth. After all, as Christians we are already recipients of the greatest gift in all creation: God's grace. We have been promised the gift of eternal life through God's only begotten Son, and we must count that gift as our most precious possession.

Rather than succumbing to the sin of envy, we should focus on the marvelous things that God has done for us—starting with Christ's sacrifice. And we must refrain from preoccupying ourselves with the blessings that God has chosen to give others.

So here's a surefire formula for a happier life (and healthier relationships): Count your own blessings and let your friends count theirs. It's the godly way to live.

> When you worry about what you don't have,
> you won't be able to enjoy what you do have.
>
> Charles Swindoll

> How can you possess the miseries of envy when you
> possess in Christ the best of all portions?
>
> C. H. Spurgeon

Remember This: Feelings of envy will rob you of happiness and peace. Don't allow yourself to be robbed.

Remember That Actions Speak Louder

For the kingdom of God is not in talk but in power.

I Corinthians 4:20 Holman CSB

The old saying is both familiar and true: actions speak louder than words. And as believers, we must beware: our actions should always give credence to the changes that Christ can make in the lives of those who walk with Him.

God calls upon each of us to act in accordance with His will and with respect for His commandments. If we are to be responsible believers, we must realize that it is never enough simply to hear the instructions of God; we must also live by them. And it is never enough to wait idly by while others do God's work here on earth; we, too, must act. Doing God's work is a responsibility that each of us must bear, and when we do, our loving Heavenly Father rewards our efforts with a bountiful harvest.

The church needs people who are doers
of the Word and not just hearers.

Warren Wiersbe

It is by acts and not by ideas that people live.

Harry Emerson Fosdick

Never fail to do something because you don't feel like it.
Sometimes you just have to do it now,
and you'll feel like it later.

Marie T. Freeman

Figuring Out Friendships: Try as we might, we
simply cannot escape the consequences of our
actions. How we behave today has a direct impact
on the rewards we will receive tomorrow. That's a
lesson that we must teach our friends by our words
and our actions, but not necessarily in that order.

Seek Strength from God

The LORD is my strength and my song;
he has become my victory.
He is my God, and I will praise him.

Exodus 15:2 NLT

Where do you and your friends go to find strength? The gym? The health food store? The espresso bar? There's a better source of strength, of course, and that source is God. He is a never-ending source of strength and courage if you call upon Him.

Have you "tapped in" to the power of God? Have you turned your life, your relationships, and your heart over to Him—or are you muddling along under your own power? The answer to this question will determine the quality of your life here on earth and the destiny of your life throughout all eternity. So start tapping in—and remember that when it comes to strength, God is the Ultimate Source.

If you are weak, limited, ordinary, you are the best material
through which God can work!

Henry Blackaby and Claude King

When God is our strength, it is strength indeed;
when our strength is our own, it is only weakness.

St. Augustine

Jesus is not a strong man making men and women
who gather around Him weak.
He is the Strong creating the strong.

E. Stanley Jones

Remember This: If you're running out of energy,
perhaps you need to slow down and have a heart-
to-heart talk with God. And while you're at it,
remember that God is bigger than your problems
. . . much bigger.

Don't Give Up on God or Yourself

Thanks be to God! He gives us the victory through our Lord Jesus Christ. Therefore, my dear brothers, stand firm. Let nothing move you. Always give yourselves fully to the work of the Lord, because you know that your labor in the Lord is not in vain.

1 Corinthians 15:57-58 NIV

Do you sincerely want to live a life that is pleasing to God? If so, you must remember that life is not a sprint, it's a marathon that calls for preparation, determination, and lots of perseverance.

Are you one of those people who doesn't give up easily, or are you quick to bail out when the going gets tough? If you've developed the unfortunate habit of giving up at the first sign of trouble, it's probably time for you to have a heart-to-heart talk with the person you see every time you look in the mirror.

Jesus finished what He began, and so should you. Despite His suffering, despite the shame of the cross, Jesus was steadfast in His faithfulness to God. You, too, must remain faithful, especially when times are tough.

Do you want to build a closer relationship with God? Then don't give up. And if you're facing a difficult situation, remember this: whatever your problem, God can handle it. Your job is to keep persevering until He does.

Keep adding, keep walking, keep advancing; do not stop, do not turn back, do not turn from the straight road.

St. Augustine

God never gives up on you, so don't you ever give up on Him.

Marie T. Freeman

Perseverance is more than endurance. It is endurance combined with absolute assurance and certainty that what we are looking for is going to happen.

Oswald Chambers

Remember This: If things don't work out at first, don't quit. If you never try, you'll never know how good you can be.

Keep Studying God's Word

Your word is a lamp to my feet and a light to my path.

Psalm 119:105 NKJV

If you and your friends want to know God, you should read the book He wrote. It's called the Bible, and it is one of the most important tools that God uses to direct your steps, to enhance your relationships, and to transform your life.

You must decide whether God's Word will be a bright spotlight that guides your path every day or a tiny night-light that occasionally flickers in the dark. The decision to study the Bible—or not—is yours and yours alone. But make no mistake: the way that you choose to use your Bible will have a profound impact on you and your loved ones. Very profound!

I suggest you discipline yourself to spend time daily
in a systematic reading of God's Word.
Make this "quiet time" a priority that nobody can change.

Warren Wiersbe

Walking in faith brings you to the Word of God.
There you will be healed, cleansed, fed,
nurtured, equipped, and matured.

Kay Arthur

The Bible is God's Word, given to us by God Himself so
we can know Him and His will for our lives.

Billy Graham

Remember This: Trust God's Word. Charles Swindoll writes, " There are four words I wish we would never forget, and they are, "God keeps his word." And remember: When it comes to studying God's Word, school is always in session.

Trust the Future to God

"I say this because I know what I am planning for you,"
says the Lord. "I have good plans for you, not plans to
hurt you. I will give you hope and a good future."

Jeremiah 29:11 NCV

How bright is your future? Well, if you're a faithful believer, God's plans for you are so bright that you'd better pack lots of sunscreen. But here's an important question: How bright do you believe your future to be? Are you expecting a terrific tomorrow, or are you dreading a terrible one? The answer you give will have a powerful impact on the way tomorrow turns out.

Do you trust in the ultimate goodness of God's plan for your life? Will you face tomorrow's challenges with optimism and hope? You should. After all, God created you for a very important reason: His reason. And you still have important work to do: His work.

Today, as you live in the present and look to the future, remember that God has an amazing plan for you. Act—and believe—accordingly.

When the train goes through a tunnel and the world
becomes dark, do you jump out? Of course not.
You sit still and trust the engineer to get you through.

Corrie ten Boom

Contentment is trusting God even when things
seem out of control.

Charles Stanley

Trust in yourself and you are doomed to disappointment;
trust in money and you may have it taken from you,
but trust in God, and you are never to be
confounded in time or eternity.

D. L. Moody

Remember This: Even when the world seems dark,
the future is bright for those who look to the Son.

Don't Get Tired of Doing the Right Thing

So we must not get tired of doing good,
for we will reap at the proper time if we don't give up.

Galatians 6:9 Holman CSB

The world you live in has a way of testing your faith, your courage, and your intentions. If you intend to follow God (and if you follow through on those intentions) you'll be rewarded . . . richly rewarded. But if you cave in at the first temptation, you're headed for trouble, and fast.

So here's a foolproof formula for building better friendships and a better life: don't ever get tired of doing the right thing. When you do, you'll discover that God never gets tired of rewarding you for doing the right thing.

Although God causes all things to work together
for good for His children, He still holds us accountable
for our behavior.

Kay Arthur

Integrity is not a given factor in everyone's life.
It is a result of self-discipline, inner trust, and a decision
to be relentlessly honest in all situations in our lives.

John Maxwell

A person who gazes and keeps on gazing at Jesus
becomes like him in appearance.

E. Stanley Jones

Figuring Out Friendships: When it comes to telling
your friends about your relationship with God . . .
your actions speak much more loudly than your
words . . . so behave accordingly.

Are You Your Own Worst Critic?

A devout life does bring wealth,
but it's the rich simplicity of being yourself before God.

I Timothy 6:6 MSG

When you feel better about yourself, you'll make better choices. But sometimes, it's hard to feel good about yourself, especially when you live in a society that keeps sending out the message that you've got to be perfect.

Are you your own worst critic? And in response to that criticism, are you constantly trying to transform yourself into a person who meets society's expectations, but not God's expectations? If so, it's time to become a little more understanding of the person you see whenever you look into the mirror.

Millions of words have been written about various ways to improve self-esteem. Yet, maintaining a healthy self-image is, to a surprising extent, a matter of doing three things: 1. Obeying God. 2. Thinking healthy thoughts. 3. Finding things to do that please your Creator and yourself. When you concentrate on these things, your self-image will tend to take care of itself.

Find satisfaction in him who made you, and only then find satisfaction in yourself as part of his creation.

St. Augustine

Give yourself a gift today: be present with yourself. God is. Enjoy your own personality. God does.

Barbara Johnson

Your self image need not be permanently damaged by the circumstances of life. It can be recast when there is an infusion of new life in Jesus Christ.

Ed Young

Figuring Out Friendships: If you're too critical of other people—or of yourself—it's time to become more forgiving and less judgmental.

Remember That You Can Have a New Beginning

Then the One seated on the throne said,
"Look! I am making everything new."

Revelation 21:5 Holman CSB

Have you been involved in behaviors that have left you feeling worse about yourself, not better? If so, today is the perfect day to start putting God first in your life.

Each new day offers countless opportunities to serve God, to seek His will, and to obey His teachings. But each day also offers countless opportunities to stray from God's commandments and to wander far from His path.

Sometimes, we make a mess of things, but God has better plans of us. And, whenever we ask Him to renew our strength and guide our steps, He does so.

So if you've made mistakes in the past, and if you want to make amends, consider this day a new beginning. Consider it a fresh start, a renewed opportunity to serve your Creator with willing hands and a loving heart. Ask God to renew your sense of purpose as He guides your steps. Today is a glorious opportunity to serve God. Seize that opportunity while you can; tomorrow may indeed be too late.

Mistakes offer the possibility for redemption and a new start in God's kingdom. No matter what you're guilty of, God can restore your innocence.

Barbara Johnson

Sometimes, we need a housecleaning of the heart.

Catherine Marshall

All the power of God—the same power that hung the stars in place and put the planets in their courses and transformed Earth—now resides in you to energize and strengthen you to become the person God created you to be.

Anne Graham Lotz

Remember This: God is in the business of making all things new…including you.

Be Patient and Trust God

Trust in him at all times, O people;
pour out your hearts to him, for God is our refuge.

Psalm 62:8 NIV

I f we believe in God, we should trust in God. Yet sometimes, when we are besieged by fears and doubts, trusting God is hard indeed.

Trusting God means trusting Him with every aspect of our lives. We must trust Him with our relationships and our finances. We must follow His commandments and pray for His guidance. When we experience the inevitable pains of life here on earth, we must accept God's will and seek His healing touch. And at times, we must be willing to wait patiently for God to reveal plans that only He can see.

Are you willing to trust God completely, or are you still sitting squarely on the spiritual fence? The answer to this question will determine the tone, the quality, and the direction of your life.

When you trust your Heavenly Father without reservation, you can be sure that, in His own fashion and in His own time, God will bless you in ways that you never could have imagined. So trust Him. And then prepare yourself for the abundance and the joy that will most certainly be yours when you do.

God never hurries. There are no deadlines against which He must work. To know this is to quiet our spirits and relax our nerves.

A. W. Tozer

Faith does not eliminate problems. Faith keeps you in a trusting relationship with God in the midst of your problems.

Henry Blackaby

Be patient. God is using today's difficulties to strengthen you for tomorrow. He is equipping you. The God who makes things grow will help you bear fruit.

Max Lucado

Remember This: Because God is trustworthy—and because He has made promises to you that He intends to keep—you are protected.

Stand Up for Your Beliefs

Since, then, you have been raised with Christ,
set your hearts on things above, where Christ is seated
at the right hand of God. Set your minds on things above,
not on earthly things.

Colossians 3:1-2 NIV

If you're willing to stand up for the things you believe in, you'll make better choices, and you'll build stronger friendships. But if you're one person on Sunday morning and a different person throughout the rest of the week, you'll be doing yourself—and your conscience—a big disservice.

The moment that you decide to stand up for your beliefs, you can no longer be a lukewarm, halfhearted Christian. And, when you are no longer a lukewarm Christian, God rejoices (and the devil doesn't).

So stand up for your beliefs. And remember this: in the battle of good versus evil, the devil never takes a day off . . . and neither should you.

What we believe determines how we behave,
and both determine what we become.

Warren Wiersbe

It is comfortable to know that we are responsible
to God and not to man. It is a small matter
to be judged of man's judgement.

Lottie Moon

The mind is a faculty, and magnificent one at that.
But the heart is the dwelling place of our true beliefs.

John Eldredge

Figuring Out Friendships: Talking about your beliefs
is easy. But, making your actions match your words
is much harder. Nevertheless, if you really want to
be honest with yourself and your friends, then you
must make your actions match your beliefs. Period.

Put Faith Above Feelings

Now the just shall live by faith.

Hebrews 10:38 NKJV

Hebrews 10:38 teaches that we should live by faith. Yet sometimes, despite our best intentions, negative feelings can rob us of the peace and abundance that would otherwise be ours through Christ. When anger or anxiety separates us from the spiritual blessings that God has in store, we must rethink our priorities and renew our faith. And we must place faith above feelings. Human emotions are highly variable, decidedly unpredictable, and often unreliable. Our emotions are like the weather, only far more fickle. So we must learn to live by faith, not by the ups and downs of our own emotional roller coasters.

Sometime during this day, you will probably be gripped by a strong negative emotion. Distrust it. Reign it in. Test it. And turn it over to God. Your emotions will inevitably change; God will not. So trust Him completely as you watch your feelings slowly evaporate into thin air—which, of course, they will.

We are to live by faith, not feelings.

Kay Arthur

Belief is not the result of an intellectual act;
it is the result of an act of my will whereby
I deliberately commit myself.

Oswald Chambers

Sometimes the very essence of faith is trusting
God in the midst of things He knows good
and well we cannot comprehend.

Beth Moore

Remember This: Do you trust Him completely? If
you genuinely trust God, it means you don't have
to understand everything.

Don't Let Your Problems Get You Down

People who do what is right may have many problems,
but the Lord will solve them all.

Psalm 34:19 NCV

All of us face those occasional days when the traffic jams and the dog gobbles up the homework. But, when we find ourselves overtaken by the frustrations of life, we must catch ourselves, take a deep breath, and lift our thoughts upward.

Although we must occasionally struggle to rise above the distractions and disappointments of tough times (or tough relationships), we need never struggle alone. God is here—eternally and faithfully, with infinite patience and love. And our friends and family members are also willing to help us restore perspective and peace to our souls. Our job is to let them.

Keep your feet on the ground, but let your heart soar as high as it will. Refuse to be average or to surrender to the chill of your spiritual environment.

A. W. Tozer

Hope looks for the good in people, opens doors for people, discovers what can be done to help, lights a candle, does not yield to cynicism. Hope sets people free.

Barbara Johnson

Just remember, every flower that ever bloomed had to go through a whole lot of dirt to get there!

Barbara Johnson

Remember This: Be a realistic optimist: Your attitude toward the future will help create your future. So think realistically about yourself and your situation while making a conscious effort to focus on hopes, not fears. When you do, you'll put the self-fulfilling prophecy to work for you.

Don't Worry So Much About "Looking Good"

He said to them, "You make yourselves look good in front of people, but God knows what is really in your hearts. What is important to people is hateful in God's sight."

Luke 16:15 NCV

You and your friends live in a society that is obsessed with "looking good." Everywhere you turn, you're confronted with a steady stream of subtle messages that try to convince you it's more important to look good than to be good. These messages are not only false, but they are also dangerous to your spiritual and emotional health.

Would you like to build a better life and stronger relationships? If so, here's a great place to start: worry less about appearances and more about substance. When you do, you may find that you're a little out of step with the world, which is perfectly okay. After all, the world sees people and things as they appear to be, but God sees them as they really are . . . and that's the way you should try to see them, too.

True friends will always lift you higher
and challenge you to walk in a manner
pleasing to our Lord.

Lisa Bevere

Those who follow the crowd usually get lost in it.

Rick Warren

You can't judge a book by its cover.

Old-time Saying

Remember This: Don't be too worried about what you look like on the outside; be more concerned about the kind of person you are on the inside. God loves you just like you are . . . and now, it's your turn to do the same thing.

Learn to Communicate

Rash language cuts and maims,
but there is healing in the words of the wise.
Proverbs 12:18 MSG

If you want to build strong friendships, you should teach yourself to become an effective communicator. And that's exactly what God wants you to do. God's Word reminds us that "Reckless words pierce like a sword, but the tongue of the wise brings healing" (Proverbs 12:18 NIV).

Today, make this promise to yourself: vow to be an honest, effective, encouraging communicator at school, at home, at church, and everyplace in between. Speak wisely, not impulsively. Use words of kindness and praise, not words of anger or derision. Learn how to be truthful without being cruel. Remember that you have the power to heal others or to injure them, to lift others up or to hold them back. And when you learn how to lift them up, you'll soon discover that you've lifted yourself up, too.

Part of good communication is listening
with the eyes as well as with the ears.

Josh McDowell

Like dynamite, God's power is only latent power
until it is released. You can release God's dynamite power
into people's lives and the world through faith,
your words, and prayer.

Bill Bright

Attitude and the spirit in which we communicate
are as important as the words we say.

Charles Stanley

Remember This: Think first, speak second: If you
blurt out the first thing that comes into your head,
you may say things that are better left unsaid.

Don't Hang Out with Cruel People

My dear friend, do not follow what is bad;
follow what is good.

3 John 1:11 NCV

Sometimes people can be cruel . . . very cruel. When other people are unkind to you or to your friends, you may be tempted to strike back, either verbally or physically. Don't do it! Instead, remember that God corrects other people's behaviors in His own way, and He doesn't need your help (even if you're totally convinced you're "in the right"). Remember that God has commanded you to forgive others, just as you, too, must sometimes seek forgiveness from others.

So, when other people behave cruelly, foolishly, or impulsively—as they will from time to time—don't start swinging or screaming. Speak up for yourself as politely as you can, and walk away. Next, forgive everybody as quickly as you can. Then, get on with your life, and leave the rest up to God.

When something robs you of your peace of mind, ask yourself if it is worth the energy you are expending on it. If not, then put it out of your mind in an act of discipline. Every time the thought of "it" returns, refuse it.

Kay Arthur

You can be sure you are abiding in Christ if you are able to have a Christlike love toward the people that irritate you the most.

Vonette Bright

A keen sense of humor helps us to overlook the unbecoming, understand the unconventional, tolerate the unpleasant, overcome the unexpected, and outlast the unbearable.

Billy Graham

Remember This: A thoughtful Christian doesn't follow the crowd . . . a thoughtful Christian follows Jesus.

Worship God Every Day

Worship the Lord your God and . . . serve Him only.
Matthew 4:10 Holman CSB

If you really want to enjoy a better life (and better relationships), here's something you can do: try worshipping God seven days a week, not just on Sundays.

God has a wonderful plan for your life, and an important part of that plan includes the time that you set aside for praise and worship. Every life, including yours, is based upon some form of worship. The question is not whether you will worship, but what you worship.

If you choose to worship God, you will receive a bountiful harvest of joy, peace, and abundance. But if you distance yourself from God by foolishly worshiping earthly possessions and personal gratification, you're making a huge mistake. So do yourself a favor: Worship God today and every day. Worship Him with sincerity and thanksgiving. Write His name on your heart and rest assured that He, too, has written your name on His.

We are never more fulfilled than when our longing for God is met by His presence in our lives.

Billy Graham

Spiritual worship is focusing all we are on all He is.

Beth Moore

Each time, before you intercede, be quiet first and worship God in His glory. Think of what He can do and how He delights to hear the prayers of His redeemed people. Think of your place and privilege in Christ, and expect great things!

Andrew Murray

Remember This: Worship is not meant to be boxed up in a church building on Sunday morning. To the contrary, praise and worship should be woven into the very fabric of your life. Do you take time each day to worship your Father in heaven, or do you wait until Sunday morning to praise Him for His blessings? The answer to this question will, in large part, determine the quality and direction of your life. So worship accordingly.

Let God Guide the Way

*The true children of God are those who let
God's Spirit lead them.*
Romans 8:14 NCV

The Bible promises that God will guide you if you let Him. Your job is to let Him. But sometimes, you will be tempted to do otherwise. Sometimes, you'll be tempted to go along with the crowd; other times, you'll be tempted to do things your way, not God's way. When you feel these temptations, resist them.

God has promised that when you ask for His help, He will not withhold it. So ask. Ask Him to meet the needs of your day. Ask Him to lead you, to protect you, and to correct you. And trust the answers He gives.

God stands at the door and waits. When you knock, He opens. When you ask, He answers. Your task, of course, is to seek His guidance prayerfully, confidently, and often.

If we want to hear God's voice,
we must surrender our minds and hearts to Him.

Billy Graham

Are you serious about wanting God's guidance to become
a personal reality in your life? The first step is to tell God
that you know you can't manage your own life;
that you need his help.

Catherine Marshall

We have ample evidence that the Lord is able to guide.
The promises cover every imaginable situation.
All we need to do is to take the hand he stretches out.

Elisabeth Elliot

Remember This: Pray for guidance. When you seek
it, He will give it.

Pay Attention to What's Happening Around You

Pay careful attention, then, to how you walk—
not as unwise people but as wise.

Ephesians 5:15 Holman CSB

You can learn a lot about life, love, and the pursuit of happiness by paying attention to the things that happen around you—so keep your eyes and ears open. And while you're at it, please try to remember that "denial" isn't a big river in Egypt (it is, in truth, the natural human tendency to ignore little problems until they grow too big to ignore).

God is trying to teach you things, and you can learn these lessons the easy way (by paying attention, by learning from other people's mistakes, and by obeying God's commandments) or the hard way (by making your own mistakes, and by continuing to make them over and over again until you finally learn something). Of course, it's better to learn things sooner rather than later . . . starting now. So what are you waiting for?

Experience has taught me that the Shepherd is far more willing to show His sheep the path than the sheep are to follow. He is endlessly merciful, patient, tender, and loving. If we, His stupid and wayward sheep, really want to be led, we will without fail be led. Of that I am sure.

Elisabeth Elliot

Believe and do what God says. The life-changing consequences will be limitless, and the results will be confidence and peace of mind.

Franklin Graham

Much guilt arises in the life of the believer from practicing the chameleon life of environmental adaptation.

Beth Moore

Figuring Out Friendships: Do you or your friends ever find yourselves getting in the same kind of trouble over and over again? If so, there are things in your lives that need to be fixed—and you've probably been trying to ignore them. Ignore no more! You'll never fix the problems that you're unwilling to acknowledge.

Remember the Golden Rule

Do to others what you want them to do to you.

Matthew 7:12 NCV

Life is simply better when when we treat other people in the same way we would want to be treated if we were in their shoes. Things go better when we're courteous and compassionate. Graciousness, humility, and kindness are all virtues we should strive for. But sometimes, we fall short. Sometimes, amid the busyness and confusion of everyday life, we may neglect to share a kind word or a kind deed. This oversight hurts others, and it hurts us as well.

Today, slow yourself down and be alert for those who need your smile, your kind words, your hug, or your helping hand. Make kindness a centerpiece of your dealings with others. They will be blessed, and you will be, too. But not necessarily in that order.

We should behave to our friends as we would wish
our friends to behave to us.

Aristotle

The Golden Rule starts at home,
but it should never stop there.

Marie T. Freeman

The golden rule to follow to obtain spiritual
understanding is not one of intellectual pursuit,
but one of obedience.

Oswald Chambers

Figuring Out Friendships: When you're trying
to decide how to treat a friend, ask yourself this
question: "How would I feel if somebody treated
me that way?" Then, treat your friend the way that
you would want to be treated.

Remember This: The Golden Rule is God's rule, and
it should be your rule, too.

Remember Christ's Love

For I am persuaded that neither death nor life,
nor angels nor principalities nor powers, nor things present
nor things to come, nor height nor depth, nor any other
created thing, shall be able to separate us from the love of
God which is in Christ Jesus our Lord.

Romans 8:38-39 NKJV

How much does Christ love us? More than we, as mere mortals, can comprehend. His love is perfect and steadfast. Even though we are imperfect and wayward, the Good Shepherd cares for us still. Even though we have fallen far short of the Father's commandments, Christ loves us with a power and depth that are beyond our understanding. The sacrifice that Jesus made upon the cross was made for each of us, and His love endures to the edge of eternity and beyond.

Christ's love changes everything, including your relationships. When you accept His gift of grace, you are transformed, not only for today, but also for all eternity.

Jesus is waiting patiently for you to invite Him into your heart. Please don't make Him wait a single minute longer.

He loved us not because we're lovable,
but because He is love.

C. S. Lewis

God expressed His love in sending
the Holy Spirit to live within us.

Charles Stanley

God is my Heavenly Father. He loves me with
an everlasting love. The proof of that is the Cross.

Elisabeth Elliot

Remember This: Jesus loves you. His love is
amazing, it's wonderful, and it's meant for you.

Remember the Importance of Courtesy

Be hospitable to one another without grumbling.

I Peter 4:9 NKJV

Did Christ instruct us in matters of etiquette and courtesy? Of course He did. Christ's instructions are clear: "In everything, therefore, treat people the same way you want them to treat you, for this is the Law and the Prophets" (Matthew 7:12 NASB). Jesus did not say, "In some things, treat people as you wish to be treated." And, He did not say, "From time to time, treat others with kindness." Christ said that we should treat others as we wish to be treated in every aspect of our daily lives. This, of course, is a tall order indeed, but as Christians, we are commanded to do our best.

Today, be a little kinder than necessary to family members, friends, and total strangers. And, as you consider all the things that Christ has done in your life, honor Him with your words and with your deeds. He expects no less, and He deserves no less.

When you extend hospitality to others,
you're not trying to impress people;
you're trying to reflect God to them.

Max Lucado

Only the courteous can love,
but it is love that makes them courteous.

C. S. Lewis

Courtesy is contagious.

Marie T. Freeman

Figuring Out Friendships: Remember, courtesy
isn't optional. If you disagree, do so without being
disagreeable; if you're angry, hold your tongue; if
you're frustrated or tired, don't argue . . . take a
nap.

Remember That Your Circumstances Change but God Does Not

The Lord is my rock, my fortress and my Savior;
my God is my rock in whom I find protection. He is my shield,
the strength of my salvation, and my stronghold.

Psalm 18:2 NLT

We live in a world that is always changing, but we worship a God that never changes—thank goodness! That means that we can be comforted in the knowledge that our Heavenly Father is the rock that simply cannot be moved: "I am the Lord, I do not change" (Malachi 3:6 NKJV).

The next time you face difficult circumstances, tough times, unfair treatment, or a broken relationship, remember that some things never change—things like the love that you feel in your heart for your family and friends . . . and the love that God feels for you. So, instead of worrying too much about life's challenges, focus your energies on finding solutions. Have faith in your own abilities, do your best to solve your problems, and leave the rest up to God.

The God who spoke still speaks.
He comes into our world. He comes into your world.
He comes to do what you can't.

Max Lucado

More often than not, when something looks like
it's the absolute end, it is really the beginning.

Charles Swindoll

God does not give us everything we want,
but He does fulfill all His promises as He leads us along
the best and straightest paths to Himself.

Dietrich Bonhoeffer

Remember This: Change is inevitable . . . you can either roll with it or be rolled over by it. Choose the former.

Always Treat Your Body with Respect

Don't you know that you are God's temple
and that God's Spirit lives in you?

I Corinthians 3:16 NCV

How do you treat your body? Do you treat it with the reverence and respect it deserves, or do you take it more or less for granted? Well, the Bible has clear instructions about the way you should take care of the miraculous body that God has given you.

God's Word teaches us that our bodies are "temples" which belong to God. We are commanded (not encouraged, not advised—commanded!) to treat our bodies with respect and honor. We do so by making wise choices and by making those choices consistently over an extended period of time.

Are you willing to treat your body with the reverence that it deserves? Then promise yourself—and God—that you will make the kind of wise choices that reflect your obedience to God's commandments. The responsibility for those choices is yours. And so are the rewards.

A Christian should no more defile his body
than a Jew would defile the temple.

Warren Wiersbe

People are funny. When they are young, they will spend
their health to get wealth. Later, they will gladly pay
all they have trying to get their health back.

John Maxwell

God wants you to give Him your body.
Some people do foolish things with their bodies.
God wants your body as a holy sacrifice.

Warren Wiersbe

Remember This: God has given you a marvelous
gift: your body. Treat it marvelously.

Learn to Say No

*Discretion will protect you
and understanding will guard you.*

Proverbs 2:11 NIV

If your friends encourage you to do things that you know are wrong, do you have enough confidence to say no? Hopefully so. But if you haven't quite learned the art of saying no, don't feel like the Lone Ranger—plenty of people much older than you still have trouble standing up for themselves.

An important part of growing up is learning how to assert yourself. Another part of growing up is learning when to say no. For most people, these are lessons that take a long time to learn, so if you're wise, you'll start learning them sooner rather than later. Remember: you have the right to say no, and you have the right to say it right now!

When your conscience says "No,"
then you must say it, too.

Criswell Freeman

Judge everything in the light of Jesus Christ.

Oswald Chambers

Life is built on character,
but character is built on decisions.

Warren Wiersbe

Remember This: If you're about to make an important decision, don't be impulsive. Remember: big decisions have big consequences, and if you don't think about those consequences now, you may pay a big price later.

Live Triumphantly

The lines of purpose in your lives never grow slack, tightly tied as they are to your future in heaven, kept taut by hope.

Colossians 1:5 MSG

Are you living the triumphant life that God has promised? Or are you, instead, a spiritual shrinking violet? As you ponder that question, consider this: God does not intend that you live a life that is commonplace or mediocre. And He doesn't want you to hide your light "under a basket." Instead, He wants you to "Let your light so shine before men, that they may see your good works and glorify your Father in heaven" (Matthew 5:16 NKJV). In short, God wants you to live a triumphant life so that others might know precisely what it means to be a believer.

The Christian life should be a triumphal celebration, a daily exercise in thanksgiving and praise. Join that celebration today. And while you're at it, make sure that you let everybody—including your friends—know that you've joined.

Continually restate to yourself what
the purpose of your life is.

Oswald Chambers

Life is a gift from God, and we must treasure it,
protect it, and invest it.

Warren Wiersbe

Jesus wants Life for us, Life with a capital L.

John Eldredge

Remember This: God still has a wonderful plan for
your life. And the time to start looking for that
plan—and living it—is now.

Stay Humble!

Humble yourselves therefore under the mighty hand of God, so that He may exalt you in due time, casting all your care upon Him, because He cares about you.

1 Peter 5:6-7 Holman CSB

On the road to spiritual and personal growth, pride is a massive roadblock. Simply put, the more prideful you are, the more difficult it is to know God.

When you experience success, it's easy to puff out your chest and proclaim, "I did that!" But it's wrong. Dietrich Bonhoeffer was correct when he observed, "It is very easy to overestimate the importance of our own achievements in comparison with what we owe others." In other words, reality breeds humility.

So if you want to know God better—and if you want to be successful in life and love—be humble. Otherwise, you'll be building a roadblock between you and your Creator (and that's a very bad thing to do!).

Nothing sets a person so much out of
the devil's reach as humility.

Jonathan Edwards

I can usually sense that a leading is from the Holy Spirit
when it calls me to humble myself, to serve somebody, to
encourage somebody, or to give something away.
Very rarely will the evil one lead us
to do those kind of things.

Bill Hybels

Do you wish to rise? Begin by descending.
You plan a tower that will pierce the clouds?
Lay first the foundation of humility.

St. Augustine

Remember This: Do you value humility above
status? If so, God will smile upon your endeavors.
But if you value status above humility, you're
inviting God's displeasure. In short, humility
pleases God; pride does not.

Friends Who Encourage You

Pleasant words are like a honeycomb,
Sweetness to the soul and health to the bones.
Proverbs 16:24 NKJV

I f you'd like to build a positive life and a positive self-image, hang out with friends who see the world—and you—in a positive light. When you do, you'll discover that good thoughts are contagious, and you can catch them from your friends.

As Christians, we have every reason to be optimistic about life. As John Calvin observed, "There is not one blade of grass, there is no color in this world that is not intended to make us rejoice." But, sometimes, rejoicing may be the last thing on our minds. Sometimes, we fall prey to worry, frustration, anxiety, or sheer exhaustion. And if we're not careful, we'll spread our pessimism to the people we love most. But God's Word instructs us to do otherwise.

In Ephesians, Paul advises, "Do not let any unwholesome talk come out of your mouths, but only what is helpful for building others up according to their needs, that it may benefit those who listen" (4:29 NIV). Paul's words still apply.

Your friends and family members probably need more encouragement and less criticism. The same can be said for you. So be a booster, not a cynic—and find friends who do likewise.

We can never untangle all the woes in other people's lives.
We can't produce miracles overnight.
But we can bring a cup of cool water to a thirsty soul,
or a scoop of laughter to a lonely heart.

Barbara Johnson

Figuring Out Friendships: Sometimes, even a very few words can make a very big difference. As Fanny Crosby observed, "A single word, if spoken in a friendly spirit, may be sufficient to turn one from dangerous error."

Be Enthusiastic

Celebrate God all day, every day. I mean, revel in him!
Philippians 4:4 MSG

Are you "burning" with enthusiasm about your life, your friends, and your future? If so, congratulations, and keep up the good work! But, if your spiritual batteries are running low, perhaps you're spending too much energy focusing on your losses and too little time planning for future victories.

Writer Sara Jordan has this simple (but effective) advice: "Every day give yourself a good mental shampoo."

So if you're feeling tired, or troubled, or both, don't despair. Instead, take time to count your blessings as you focus on things positive. And while you're at it, seek strength from the Source that never fails. When you sincerely petition God, He will give you all the strength you need to live victoriously through Him.

There seems to be a chilling fear of holy enthusiasm among the people of God. We try to tell how happy we are—but we remain so well-controlled that there are very few waves of glory experienced in our midst.

A. W. Tozer

When we wholeheartedly commit ourselves to God, there is nothing mediocre or run-of-the-mill about us. To live for Christ is to be passionate about our Lord and about our lives.

Jim Gallery

One of the great needs in the church today is for every Christian to become enthusiastic about his faith in Jesus Christ.

Billy Graham

Remember This: If you become excited about life . . . life will become an exciting adventure.

Don't Indulge in Gossip

A useless person causes trouble,
and a gossip ruins friendships.

Proverbs 16:28 NCV

Face it: gossip is bad—and the Bible clearly tells us that gossip is wrong.

When we say things that we don't want other people to know we said, we're being somewhat dishonest, but if the things we say aren't true, we're being very dishonest. Either way, we have done something that we may regret later, especially when the other person finds out.

So do yourself a big favor: don't gossip. It's a waste of words, and it's the wrong thing to do. You'll feel better about yourself if you don't gossip (and other people will feel better about you, too). So don't do it!

The great test of a man's character is his tongue.
Oswald Chambers

We are in a continual battle with the spiritual forces of evil, but we will triumph when we yield to God's leading and call on His powerful presence in prayer.
Shirley Dobson

The cost of gossip always exceeds its worth.
Jim Gallery

Figuring Out Friendships: Watch what you say. Don't say something behind someone's back that you wouldn't say to that person directly.

Integrity Matters

A good name is to be chosen over great wealth.

Proverbs 22:1 Holman CSB

Hey, would you like a time-tested, ironclad formula for successful friendships? Here it is: guard your integrity like you guard your wallet.

It has been said on many occasions and in many ways that honesty is the best policy. For Christians, it is far more important to note that honesty is God's policy. And if we are to be servants worthy of our Savior, Jesus Christ, we must be honest, forthright, and trustworthy.

Telling the truth means telling the whole truth. And that means summoning the courage to deliver bad news when necessary. And for some of us, especially those of us who are card-carrying people pleasers, telling the whole truth can be difficult indeed (especially if we're pretty sure that the truth will make somebody mad). Still, if we wish to fashion successful lives, we've got to learn to be totally truthful—part-time truth-telling doesn't cut the mustard.

Sometimes, honesty is difficult; sometimes, honesty is painful; sometimes, honesty is inconvenient; but honesty is always God's way. In the Book of Proverbs, we read, "The

Lord detests lying lips, but he delights in men who are truthful" (12:22 NIV). Clearly, truth is God's way, and it must be our way, too, even when telling the truth is difficult.

Integrity is a sign of maturity.
Charles Swindoll

There's nothing like the power of integrity.
It is a characteristic so radiant, so steady, so consistent,
so beautiful, that it makes a permanent
picture in our minds.
Franklin Graham

Integrity of heart is indispensable.
John Calvin

Remember This: You can always remove yourself from situations that might compromise your integrity.

Take Your Concerns to God

*Cast your burden on the Lord, and He will support you;
He will never allow the righteous to be shaken.*

Psalm 55:22 Holman CSB

The Bible promises this: tough times are temporary but God's love is not—God's love endures forever. So what does that mean to you? Just this: From time to time, everybody faces disappointments and broken relationships—so will you. And when tough times arrive, God always stands ready to protect you and to heal you. Your task is straightforward: you must share your burdens with Him.

As Corrie ten Boom observed, "Any concern that is too small to be turned into a prayer is too small to be made into a burden." Those are comforting words, especially during difficult days.

Whatever the size of your challenges, God is big enough to handle them. Ask for His help today, with faith and with fervor. Instead of turning things over in your mind, turn them over to God in prayer. Instead of worrying about your next decision, ask God to lead the way. Cast your burdens upon the One who cannot be shaken, and rest assured that He always hears your prayers.

Claim all of God's promises in the Bible. Your sins, your worries, your life—you may cast them all on Him.
Corrie ten Boom

Our fears for today, our worries about tomorrow, and even the powers of hell can't keep God's love away.
Bill Bright

Anxiety does not empty tomorrow of its sorrows, but it empties today of its strength.
C. H. Spurgeon

Remember This: Assiduously divide your areas of concern into two categories: those you can control and those you cannot. Resolve never to waste time or energy worrying about the latter.

Make God the Cornerstone

Because the eyes of the Lord are on the righteous
and His ears are open to their request.
But the face of the Lord is against those who do evil.

1 Peter 3:12 Holman CSB

Have you made God the cornerstone of your life and your relationships, or is He relegated to a few hours on Sunday morning? Have you genuinely allowed God to reign over every corner of your heart, or have you attempted to place Him in a spiritual compartment? The answer to these questions will determine the direction of your day and your life.

God loves you. In times of trouble, He will comfort you; in times of sorrow, He will dry your tears. When you are weak or sorrowful, God is as near as your next breath. He stands at the door of your heart and waits. Welcome Him in and allow Him to rule. And then, accept the peace, and the strength, and the protection, and the abundance that only God can give.

I have so much to do that I shall spend
the first three hours of the day in prayer.

Martin Luther

God is everything. My focus must be on him,
seeking to know him more completely
and allowing him full possession of my life.

Mary Morrison Suggs

Prayer does not fit us for the greater work;
prayer is the greater work.

Oswald Chambers

Remember This: Finding time for God takes time . . .
and it's up to you to find it. The world is constantly
vying for your attention, and sometimes the noise
can be deafening. Remember the words of Elisabeth
Elliot; she said, "The world is full of noise. Let us
learn the art of silence, stillness, and solitude."

Find Friends Who Pay Attention to God

Your heart will be where your treasure is.

Luke 12:34 NCV

Jesus deserves your undivided attention. Are you and your friends giving it to Him? Hopefully so.

When you focus your thoughts and prayers on the One from Galilee, you'll start building a better life and better relationships. But beware: the world will try to convince you that "other things" are more important than your faith. These messages are both false and dangerous—don't believe them.

When it comes to your spiritual, emotional, and personal growth, absolutely nothing is more important than your faith. So do yourself and your loved ones a favor: focus on God and His only begotten Son. Your loved ones will be glad you did . . . and so will you.

He doesn't need an abundance of words.
He doesn't need a dissertation about your life.
He just wants your attention. He wants your heart.

Kathy Troccoli

Make a plan now to keep a daily appointment with God.
The enemy is going to tell you to set it aside, but you must
carve out the time. If you're too busy to meet with
the Lord, friend, then you are simply too busy.

Charles Swindoll

Jesus: the proof of God's love.

Philip Yancey

Remember This: The world wants you to focus on
"stuff." God wants you to focus on His Son. Trust
God.

Share Your Faith

And I say to you, anyone who acknowledges Me before men,
the Son of Man will also acknowledge him before
the angels of God; but whoever denies Me before men
will be denied before the angels of God.

Luke 12:8-9 Holman CSB

Genuine faith was never meant to be locked up in the heart of a believer—to the contrary, it is meant to be shared with the world. But, if you sincerely wish to share your faith, you must first find it.

How can you find and strengthen your faith? Through praise, through worship, through fellowship, through Bible study, and through prayer. When you do these things, your faith will become stronger, and you will find ways to share your beliefs with your family, with your friends, and with the world. And when you do, everybody wins.

To take up the cross means that you take your stand
for the Lord Jesus no matter what it costs.

Billy Graham

Usually it is those who know Him that bring Him to
others. That is why the Church, the whole body of
Christians showing Him to one another, is so important.

C. S. Lewis

Our Lord is searching for people who will make
a difference. Christians dare not dissolve into
the background or blend into the neutral
scenery of the world.

Charles Swindoll

Figuring Out Friendships: If your eternity with God
is secure (because you believe in Jesus), you have
a profound responsibility to tell as many friends as
you can about the eternal life that Christ offers to
those who believe in Him.

Nurture Your Relationship with God

Be silent before the Lord and wait expectantly for Him.

Psalm 37:7 Holman CSB

Are you willing to place God first in your life? And, are you willing to welcome God's Son into your heart? Unless you can honestly answer these questions with a resounding yes, then your relationship with God isn't what it could be or should be.

As you think about the nature of your relationship with God, remember this: you will always have some type of relationship with Him—it is inevitable that your life must be lived in relationship to God. The question is not if you will have a relationship with Him; the burning question is whether or not that relationship will be one that seeks to honor Him . . . or not.

Thankfully, God is always available, He's always ready to forgive, and He's waiting to hear from you now. The rest, of course, is up to you.

Although God most assuredly wills
that His children study Scripture thoroughly,
scholarship is not His main goal for us.
Relationship is.

Beth Moore

Speed-reading may be a good thing, but it was never
meant for the Bible. It takes calm, thoughtful,
prayerful meditation on the Word to extract
its deepest nourishment.

Vance Havner

Remember This: Do you try to spend quiet
moments with God every day of the week? If so,
keep it up. If not, why not?

Remember That Sin Enslaves

Jesus responded, "I assure you:
Everyone who commits sin is a slave of sin."
John 8:34 Holman CSB

Because we are creatures of free will, we may disobey God whenever we choose. But when we do so, we put ourselves and our loved ones in peril. Why? Because disobedience invites disaster. We cannot sin against God without consequences. We cannot live outside His will without injury. We cannot distance ourselves from God without hardening our hearts. We cannot yield to the ever-tempting distractions of our world and, at the same time, enjoy God's peace.

Sometimes, in a futile attempt to justify our behaviors, we make a distinction between "big" sins and "little" ones. To do so is a mistake of "big" proportions. Sins of all shapes and sizes have the power to do us great harm. And in a world where sin is big business, that's certainly a sobering thought.

Before we can be filled with the Living Water,
we must be cleansed of sin. Before we can be
cleansed of sin, we must be convicted.
And sometimes it's painful. And shameful.

Anne Graham Lotz

We cannot out-sin God's ability to forgive us.

Beth Moore

He loved us even while we were yet sinners
at war with Him!

Bill Bright

Remember This: Sometimes immorality is obvious
and sometimes it's not. So beware: the most subtle
forms of sin are often the most dangerous.

Be Still

Be still, and know that I am God.
Psalm 46:10 NKJV

The Bible teaches that a wonderful way to get to know God is simply to be still and listen to Him. But sometimes, you may find it hard to slow down and listen.

As the demands of everyday life weigh down upon you, you may be tempted to ignore God's presence or—worse yet—to rebel against His commandments. But, when you quiet yourself and acknowledge His presence, God touches your heart, restores your spirits, and gives you the perspective you need to make good decisions. So why not let Him do it right now? If you really want to get to know your Heavenly Father, silence is a wonderful place to start.

Instead of waiting for the feeling, wait upon God.
You can do this by growing still and quiet, then expressing
in prayer what your mind knows is true about Him,
even if your heart doesn't feel it at this moment.

Shirley Dobson

If you, too, will learn to wait upon God, to get alone with
Him, and remain silent so that you can hear His voice
when He is ready to speak to you, what a difference
it will make in your life!

Kay Arthur

Be still: pause and discover that God is God.

Charles Swindoll

Remember This: Want to talk to God? Then don't make Him shout. If you really want to hear from God, go to a quiet place and listen. If you keep listening long enough and carefully enough, He'll start talking.

Take Time to Praise Him!

I will praise You with my whole heart.

Psalm 138:1 NKJV

If you're like most folks on the planet, you're a very busy person. Your life is probably hectic, demanding, and complicated. And when the demands of life leave you rushing from place to place with scarcely a moment to spare, you may not take time to praise your Creator. Big mistake.

The Bible makes it clear: it pays to praise God. Worship and praise should be a part of everything you do. Otherwise, you quickly lose perspective as you fall prey to the demands of everyday life.

Do you sincerely desire to know God in a more meaningful way? Then praise Him for who He is and for what He has done for you. And please don't wait until Sunday morning—praise Him all day long, every day, for as long as you live . . . and then for all eternity.

Praise—lifting up our heart and hands,
exulting with our voices, singing his praises—
is the occupation of those who dwell in the kingdom.

Max Lucado

Words fail to express my love for this holy Book,
my gratitude for its author, for His love and goodness.
How shall I thank him for it?

Lottie Moon

A child of God should be a visible beatitude for joy
and a living doxology for gratitude.

C. H. Spurgeon

Remember This: One of the big reasons you should attend church is to praise God. But, you need not wait until Sunday rolls around to thank your Heavenly Father. Instead, you can praise Him many times each day by saying silent prayers that only He can hear.

Choose Wise Role Models

Spend time with the wise and you will become wise.

Proverbs 13:20 NCV

Here's a simple yet effective way to strengthen your faith and your relationships: Choose role models whose faith in God is strong.

When you emulate godly people, you become a more godly person yourself. That's why you should seek out mentors who, by their words and their presence, make you a better person and a better Christian.

Today, as a gift to yourself, select, from your friends and family members, a mentor whose judgment you trust. Then listen carefully to your mentor's advice and be willing to accept that advice, even if accepting it requires effort, or pain, or both. Consider your mentor to be God's gift to you. Thank God for that gift, and use it for the glory of His kingdom.

The effective mentor strives to help a man or woman discover what they can be in Christ and then holds them accountable to become that person.

Howard Hendricks

God guides through the counsel of good people.

E. Stanley Jones

It takes a wise person to give good advice, but an even wiser person to take it.

Marie T. Freeman

Remember This: Your mentors may not have all of the answers, but at least they'll know most of the questions! So ask, listen, and learn.

Too Much Media?

*Let no one deceive himself. If anyone among you seems
to be wise in this age, let him become a fool that
he may become wise. For the wisdom of this world is
foolishness with God. For it is written,
"He catches the wise in their own craftiness."*

I Corinthians 3:18–19 NKJV

Sometimes it's hard being a Christian, especially when
the world keeps pumping out messages that are contrary to your faith.

The media is working around the clock in an attempt
to rearrange your priorities and your friends priorities. The
media says that your appearance is all-important, that your
clothes are all-important, that your car is all-important,
and that partying is all-important. But guess what? Those
messages are lies. The important things in your life have
little to do with parties or appearances. The all-important
things in life have to do with your faith, your family, and
your future. Period.

Are you willing to stand up for your faith? If so, you'll be
doing yourself a king-sized favor. And consider this: When
you begin to speak up for God, isn't it logical to assume that

you'll also begin to know Him in a more meaningful way? Of course you will.

So do yourself a favor: forget the media hype, and pay attention to God. Stand up for Him and be counted, not just in church where it's relatively easy to be a Christian, but also outside the church, where it's significantly harder. You owe it God . . . and you owe it to yourself.

What is courage? It is the ability to be strong in trust, in conviction, in obedience. To be courageous is to step out in faith—to trust and obey, no matter what.

Kay Arthur

Remember This: Compare the amount of time you spend watching TV to the time you spend studying God's Word. If you don't like the results of that comparison, it's time to think long and hard about the difference between the media's priorities and God's priorities.

Take the Positive Path

But the path of the just is like the shining sun, that shines ever brighter unto the perfect day. The way of the wicked is like darkness; they do not know what makes them stumble.

Proverbs 4:18-19 NKJV

When Jesus addressed His disciples, He warned that each one must, "take up his cross and follow me." The disciples must have known exactly what the Master meant. In Jesus' day, prisoners were forced to carry their own crosses to the location where they would be put to death. Thus, Christ's message was clear: in order to follow Him, Christ's disciples must deny themselves and, instead, trust Him completely. Nothing has changed since then.

If we are to be dutiful disciples of the One from Galilee, we must trust Him and we must follow Him. Jesus never comes "next." He is always first. He shows us the path of life.

Do you seek to be a worthy disciple of Jesus? Then pick up His cross today and follow in His footsteps. When you do, you can walk with confidence: He will never lead you astray.

To a world that was spiritually dry and populated with parched lives scorched by sin, [Jesus] was the Living Water who would quench the thirsty soul, saving it from "bondage" and filling it with satisfaction and joy and purpose and meaning.

Anne Graham Lotz

If doing a good act in public will excite others to do more good, then "Let your Light shine to all." Miss no opportunity to do good.

John Wesley

When we truly walk with God throughout our day, life slowly starts to fall into place.

Bill Hybels

Remember This: Following Christ is a daily journey. When you decide to walk in the footsteps of the Master, that means that you're agreeing to be a disciple seven days a week, not just on Sunday.

Be Careful How You Direct Your Thoughts

Finally brothers, whatever is true, whatever is honorable, whatever is just, whatever is pure, whatever is lovely, whatever is commendable—if there is any moral excellence and if there is any praise—dwell on these things.

Philippians 4:8 Holman CSB

How will you direct your thoughts today? Will you obey the words of Philippians 4:8 by dwelling upon those things that are honorable, pure, and worthy of praise? Or will you allow your thoughts to be hijacked by the negativity that seems to dominate our troubled world.

Are you fearful, angry, bored, or worried? Are you so preoccupied with the concerns of this day that you fail to thank God for the promise of eternity? Are you confused, bitter, or pessimistic? If so, God wants to have a little talk with you. He wants to remind you of His infinite love and His boundless grace. As you contemplate these things, and as you give thanks for God's blessings, negativity should no longer dominate your day or your life.

As we have by faith said no to sin, so we should by faith
say yes to God and set our minds on things above,
where Christ is seated in the heavenlies.

Vonette Bright

Attitude is the mind's paintbrush;
it can color any situation.

Barbara Johnson

People who do not develop and practice
good thinking often find themselves at the mercy
of their circumstances.

John Maxwell

Remember This: Good thoughts can lead you to
some very good places . . . and bad thoughts can
lead elsewhere. So guard your thoughts accordingly.

Put Holiness Before Happiness

*Blessed are those who hunger and thirst for righteousness,
because they will be filled.*

Matthew 5:6 Holman CSB

Because you are an imperfect human being, you are
not "perfectly" happy, and you won't have "perfect"
relationships—and that's perfectly okay with God.
He is far less concerned with your happiness than He is
with your holiness.

God continuously reveals Himself in everyday life, but
He does not do so in order to make you contented; He does
so in order to lead you to His Son. So don't be overly concerned with your current level of happiness: it will change.
Be more concerned with the current state of your relationship with Christ: He does not change. And because your
Savior transcends time and space, you can be comforted in
the knowledge that in the end, His joy will become your joy
. . . for all eternity.

The destined end of man is not happiness, nor health, but holiness. God's one aim is the production of saints. He is not an eternal blessing machine for men; he did not come to save men out of pity; he came to save men because he had created them to be holy.

Oswald Chambers

You don't have to be like the world to have an impact on the world. You don't have to be like the crowd to change the crowd. You don't have to lower yourself down to their level to lift them up to your level. Holiness doesn't seek to be odd. Holiness seeks to be like God.

Max Lucado

Remember This: God is holy and wants you to be holy. Christ died to make you holy. Make sure that your response to Christ's sacrifice is worthy of Him.

Place a High Value on Yourself and Your Gifts

I remind you to keep ablaze the gift of God that is in you.

2 Timothy 1:6 Holman CSB

Face it: you've got an array of talents that need to be refined. All people possess special gifts—bestowed from the Father above—and you are no exception. But, your gift is no guarantee of success; it must be cultivated—by you—or it will go unused . . . and God's gift to you will be squandered.

Today, make a promise to yourself that you will earnestly seek to discover the talents that God has given you. Then, nourish those talents and make them grow. Finally, vow to share your gifts with the world for as long as God gives you the power to do so. After all, the best way to say "Thank You" for God's gifts is to use them.

You are a unique blend of talents, skills, and gifts,
which makes you an indispensable member
of the body of Christ.

Charles Stanley

Natural abilities are like natural plants;
they need pruning by study.

Francis Bacon

You are the only person on earth
who can use your ability.

Zig Ziglar

Remember This: If you want to get better at
something, practice a little. If you want to be
outstanding, practice a lot.

Lasting Relationships Are Built upon Trust

*These are the things you must do: Speak truth to one another;
render honest and peaceful judgments in your gates.*

Zechariah 8:16 Holman CSB

L asting relationships are built upon honesty and trust.
Without trust, people soon drift apart. But with
trust, relationships grow and flourish.

As Christians, we should always try to be trustworthy,
encouraging, and loyal. And, we should be thankful for the
people who are loyal to us.

Do you want friends you can trust? Then start by being
a friend they can trust. And do you want to build relationships that stand the test of time? Then build them on a firm
foundation of trust—no shaky foundations, please!

Horizontal relationships—relationships between people—
are crippled at the outset unless
the vertical relationship—the relationship between
each person and God—is in place.

Ed Young

Whatever you do when conflicts arise, be wise.
Fight against jumping to quick conclusions and seeing
only your side. There are always two sides
on the streets of conflict. Look both ways.

Charles Swindoll

The single most important element in any human
relationship is honesty—with oneself,
with God, and with others.

Catherine Marshall

Figuring Out Friendships: Trust is the foundation
of meaningful relationships. If you want your
friendships to last, be honest and trustworthy. If
you want second- or third-class relationships, be
deceptive, evasive, and sneaky.

Have a Healthy Fear of God

Since we are receiving a Kingdom that cannot be destroyed, let us be thankful and please God by worshiping him with holy fear and awe.

Hebrews 12:28 NLT

D o you possess a healthy, fearful respect for God's power? Hopefully so. After all, the lesson from the Book of Proverbs is clear: "The fear of the Lord is the beginning of knowledge, but fools despise wisdom and instruction" (1:7 NKJV). Yet, you live in a world that often ignores the role that God plays in shaping the affairs of mankind. You live in a world where too many people consider it "unfashionable" or "unseemly" to discuss the fear of God. Don't count yourself among their number.

God maintains absolute sovereignty over His creation and His power is beyond comprehension. As believers, we must cultivate a sincere respect for God's awesome power. The fear of the Lord is, indeed, the beginning of knowledge. So today, as you face the realities of everyday life, remember this: until you acquire a healthy, respectful fear of God's power, your education is incomplete, and so is your faith.

When true believers are awed by the greatness of God
and by the privilege of becoming His children,
then they become sincerely motivated,
effective evangelists.

Bill Hybels

A healthy fear of God will do much to deter us from sin.

Charles Swindoll

The fear of God is the death of every other fear.

C. H. Spurgeon

Remember This: It's the right kind of fear: Your
respect for God should make you fearful of
disobeying Him . . . very fearful.

Remember That You Can Always Escape Temptation

The Lord knows how to deliver the godly out of temptations.

2 Peter 2:9 NKJV

If you feel like you're being boxed in by temptations, remember this: you're never completely trapped—there's always an escape hatch. And how, you ask, can you find the way out? Well, you can start by talking to God.

Beth Moore observed, "Because Christ has faced our every temptation without sin, we never face a temptation that has no door of escape." Her words apply to you.

So the next time you face a strong urge to do something wrong, slow yourself down and have a little chat with your Creator. When you talk to Him—sincerely, prayerfully, and as often as necessary—you can overcome any temptation. No exceptions.

Man without God is always torn between two urges.
His nature prompts him to do wrong,
and his conscience urges him to do right.
Christ can rid you of that inner conflict.

Billy Graham

Instant intimacy is one of the leading
warning signals of a seduction.

Beth Moore

Flee temptation without leaving a forwarding address.

Barbara Johnson

Remember This: If you're tempted to do something
you know isn't right, spend just five minutes
praying about it, and then see if you feel the same
level of temptation after you've finished praying.

Be Determined to Overcome the World

For whatever is born of God overcomes the world.
And this is the victory that has
overcome the world—our faith.

I John 5:4 NKJV

We live in the world, but we should not worship it—yet at every turn, or so it seems, we are tempted to do otherwise. As Warren Wiersbe correctly observed, "Because the world is deceptive, it is dangerous."

The 21st-century world we live in is a noisy, distracting place, a place that offers countless temptations and dangers. The world seems to cry, "Worship me with your time, your money, your energy, your thoughts, and your life!" But if we are wise, we won't fall prey to that temptation.

C. S. Lewis said, "Aim at heaven and you will get earth thrown in; aim at earth and you will get neither." That's good advice. You're likely to hit what you aim at, so aim high . . . aim at heaven.

The world's sewage system threatens to contaminate
the stream of Christian thought.
Is the world shaping your mind, or is Christ?

Billy Graham

Nothing is more foolish than a security built
upon the world and its promises,
for they are all vanity and a lie.

Matthew Henry

A fish would never be happy living on land, because it
was made for water. An eagle could never feel satisfied
if it wasn't allowed to fly. You will never feel completely
satisfied on earth, because you were made for more.

Rick Warren

Remember This: The world's power to distract,
detour, and destroy is formidable. Thankfully, God's
power is even greater.

Think Ahead

The sensible see danger and take cover;
the foolish keep going and are punished.

Proverbs 27:12 Holman CSB

If you continue to hang out with people who behave foolishly or impulsively, then sooner or later, you'll probably find yourself doing impulsive things, too. And that's bad . . . very bad. So here's an ironclad rule for maintaining your self-respect, your health, and your sanity: If you find yourself out with friends who are pressuring you to betray your values, go home and go home fast. Otherwise, before you know it, you'll be in more trouble than you can imagine.

When you feel pressured to do things—or to compromise yourself—in ways that lead you away from God, you're heading straight for major-league problems. The best time to decide how you'll behave yourself is before you go out with friends. So don't do the "easy" thing and don't do the impulsive thing. Do the right thing, and do it every time.

There may be no trumpet sound or loud applause
when we make a right decision,
just a calm sense of resolution and peace.

Gloria Gaither

Obedience is the outward expression of your love of God.

Henry Blackaby

Sin always robs us; obedience always enriches us.

Warren Wiersbe

Remember This: If you can't seem to put the brakes
on impulsive behavior . . . you're not praying hard
enough.

Don't Give in to Pessimism

Give your worries to the Lord, and he will take care of you.
He will never let good people down.

Psalm 55:22 NCV

Pessimism and Christianity don't mix. Why? Because Christians have every reason to be optimistic about life here on earth and life eternal. As C. H. Spurgeon observed, "Our hope in Christ for the future is the mainstream of our joy." But sometimes, we fall prey to worry, frustration, anxiety, or sheer exhaustion, and our hearts become heavy. What's needed is plenty of rest, a large dose of perspective, and God's healing touch, but not necessarily in that order.

Today, make this promise to yourself and keep it: vow to be a hope-filled Christian. Think optimistically about your life, your studies, and your future. Trust your hopes, not your fears. Take time to celebrate God's glorious creation. And then, when you've filled your heart with hope and gladness, share your optimism with your friends and loved ones. They'll be better for it, and so will you. But not necessarily in that order.

A pessimist is someone who believes that when
her cup runneth over she'll need a mop.

Barbara Johnson

To lose heart is to lose everything.

John Eldredge

Never yield to gloomy anticipation.
Place your hope and confidence in God.
He has no record of failure.

Mrs. Charles E. Cowman

Remember This: If you genuinely believe that God is
good, that His Son died for your sins, how can you
be pessimistic about your future? The answer, of
course, is that you can't!

Do the Right Thing

Knowing what is right is like deep water in the heart;
a wise person draws from the well within.

Proverbs 20:5 MSG

If you want to know God, you should obey God. But obeying Him isn't always easy. You live in a world that presents countless temptations to stray far from God's path. So here's some timely advice: when you're confronted with sin, walk—or better yet run—in the opposite direction.

When you seek righteousness for yourself—and when we seek the companionship of people who do likewise—you will reap the spiritual rewards that God has in store for you. When you live in accordance with God's commandments, you will be blessed. When you genuinely seek to follow in the footsteps of God's Son, you will experience God's presence, God's peace, and God's abundance.

So make yourself this promise: Support only those activities that further God's kingdom and your own spiritual growth. Then, prepare to reap the blessings that God has promised to all those who live according to His will and His Word.

A pure theology and a loose morality will never mix.

C. H. Spurgeon

What you do reveals what you believe about God,
regardless of what you say. When God reveals what
He has purposed to do, you face a crisis—a decision time.
God and the world can tell from your response what you
really believe about God.

Henry Blackaby

Discrepancies between values and practices
create chaos in a person's life.

John Maxwell

Remember This: When it comes to doing the right
thing, don't put it off. If you're not willing to do the
right thing today, why should you (or anybody else,
for that matter) expect you to change tomorrow?

When It Comes to Sin, Don't Be Neutral

*So put to death the sinful, earthly things lurking within you.
Have nothing to do with sexual sin, impurity, lust, and
shameful desires. Don't be greedy for the good things
of this life, for that is idolatry. God's terrible anger
will come upon those who do such things.*

Colossians 3:5-6 NLT

Nineteenth-century clergyman Edwin Hubbel Chapin warned, "Neutral men are the devil's allies." His words were true then, and they're true now. Neutrality in the face of evil is a sin. Yet all too often, we fail to fight evil, not because we are neutral, but because we are shortsighted: we don't fight the devil because we don't recognize his handiwork.

If we are to recognize evil and fight it, we must pay careful attention. We must pay attention to God's Word, and we must pay attention to the realities of everyday life. When we observe life objectively, and when we do so with eyes and hearts that are attuned to God's Holy Word, we can no longer be neutral believers. And when we are no longer neutral, God rejoices while the devil despairs.

The greatest enemy of holiness is not passion;
it is apathy.

John Eldredge

Jesus calls you to be a non-conformist.
Live to be separated from the evils of the world.
Live to be different.

Billy Graham

The greatest need a person has is not physical healing but
spiritual healing. Sin ravages the soul far worse
than disease ravages the body.

Warren Wiersbe

Remember This: Evil does exist, and you will
confront it. Prepare yourself by forming a genuine,
life-changing relationship with God and His only
begotten Son.

Keep Your Heart Pure

Everything is pure to those whose hearts are pure.
But nothing is pure to those who are corrupt and unbelieving,
because their minds and consciences are defiled.

Titus 1:15 NLT

You are near and dear to God. He loves you more than you can imagine, and He wants the very best for you. And one more thing: God wants you to guard your heart.

Every day, you are faced with choices . . . lots of them. You can do the right thing, or not. You can tell the truth, or not. You can be kind, and generous, and obedient. Or not.

Today, the world will offer you countless opportunities to let down your guard and, by doing so, let the devil do his worst. Be watchful and obedient. Guard your heart by giving it to your Heavenly Father; it is safe with Him.

Religious activity can never substitute for a heart
that is pure before Him.

Henry Blackaby

Those whose hearts are pure are the temples
of the Holy Spirit.

Luci Swindoll

Spiritual truth is discernible only to a pure heart,
not to a keen intellect. It is not a question of profundity of
intellect, but of purity of heart.

Oswald Chambers

Remember This: God loves you for who you are,
not because of the things you've done. So open
your heart to God's love . . . when you do, you'll
feel better about everything, including yourself.

Don't Underestimate the Importance of Your Friends

As iron sharpens iron, a friend sharpens a friend.

Proverbs 27:17 NLT

Are your closest friends the kind of people who encourage you to behave yourself? And are you a better person because of those friendships? If so, you've chosen your friends wisely.

But if your friends encourage you to do things that you know to be wrong, perhaps it's time to think long and hard about procuring some new pals.

Whether you realize it or not, you're probably going to behave like your friends behave. So pick out friends who make you want to become a better person. When you do, you'll be saving yourself from a lot of trouble . . . make that a whole lot of trouble.

Friendship is the greatest of worldly goods. Certainly to me it is the chief happiness of life. If I had to give a piece of advice to a young man about a place to live, I think I should say, "sacrifice almost everything to live where you can be near your friends." I know I am very fortunate in that respect.

C. S. Lewis

Yes, the Spirit was sent to be our Counselor. Yes, Jesus speaks to us personally. But often He works through another human being.

John Eldredge

A friend is one who makes me do my best.

Oswald Chambers

Figuring Out Friendships: Your friends will have a major impact on your self-image. That's an important reason (but not the only reason) to select your friends carefully.

Remember That God Is Watching

I always do my best to have a clear conscience toward God and men.

Acts 24:16 Holman CSB

You can keep some secrets from other people, but you can't keep any secrets from God. God knows what you think and what you do. And, if you want to please Him, you must start with good intentions and a pure heart.

If your heart tells you not to do something, don't do it! If your conscience tells you that something is wrong, stop! If you feel ashamed by something you've done, don't do it ever again! And if your spirit is being crushed by a relationship you're in, escape!

And while you're at it, don't do anything that you wouldn't do if God were standing right behind you, looking over your shoulder . . . because He is.

God cannot lead the individual who is not willing to give Him a blank check with his life.

Catherine Marshall

True faith commits us to obedience.

A. W. Tozer

God grades on the cross, not the curve.

Anonymous

Remember This: Of course we know that God watches over us, but we must also make certain that our friends know that we know. And, we must behave in ways that let our friends know that we know that He knows. Whew!

Get Wisdom, Be Happy

*To acquire wisdom is to love oneself; people who cherish
understanding will prosper.*

Proverbs 19:8 NLT

Are you and your friends wise guys (and girls)? And,
are you striving to help each other become a little
wiser every day? Hopefully so.

All of us would like to be wise, but not all of us are willing to do the work that is required to become wise. Why?
Because wisdom isn't free—it takes time and effort to acquire.

To become wise, we must seek God's wisdom and live
according to His Word. To become wise, we must seek wisdom with consistency and purpose. To become wise, we
must not only learn the lessons of the Christian life, we
must also live by them (and hang out with people who do
likewise).

If you sincerely desire to become wise—and if you
seek to share your hard-earned wisdom with others—your
actions must give credence to your words. The best way
to share one's wisdom—perhaps the only way—is not by
words, but by example.

Wisdom is like a savings account: If you add to it consistently, then eventually you'll have a great sum. The secret to success is consistency. Do you seek wisdom? Then seek it every day, and seek it in the right place. That place, of course, is, first and foremost, the Word of God.

Wisdom is the God-given ability to see life
with rare objectivity and to handle life
with rare stability.

Charles Swindoll

This is my song through endless ages:
Jesus led me all the way.

Fanny Crosby

Remember This: Don't be satisfied with the acquisition of knowledge . . . strive to acquire wisdom. As Beth Moore correctly observed, "A big difference exists between a head full of knowledge and the words of God literally abiding in us."

Have a Chat with God Every Morning

Morning by morning he wakens me and opens
my understanding to his will.
The Sovereign Lord has spoken to me, and I have listened.
Isaiah 50:4-5 NLT

D o you want to know God better? And do you want to let Him help you build strong, healthy relationships? Then schedule a meeting with Him every day.

Daily life is a tapestry of habits, and no habit is more important to your spiritual health than the discipline of daily prayer and devotion to the Creator. When you begin each day with your head bowed and your heart lifted, you are reminded of God's love and God's laws.

When you do engage in a regular regime of worship and praise, God will reward you for your wisdom and your obedience.

A person with no devotional life generally struggles
with faith and obedience.

Charles Stanley

The moment you wake up each morning, all your wishes
and hopes for the day rush at you like wild animals.
And the first job each morning consists in shoving it all
back; in listening to that other voice, taking that other
point of view, letting that other, larger, stronger,
quieter life coming flowing in.

C. S. Lewis

Devotional books have an important ministry,
but they are never substitutes for your Bible.

Warren Wiersbe

Remember This: The right way to start the day?
Begin it with a few minutes of quiet time to
organize your thoughts. During this time, read at
least one uplifting Bible passage and thus begin
your day on a positive, productive note.

When It Comes to Your Friendships, Your Choices Have Major Consequences

Wisdom is pleasing to you. If you find it,
you have hope for the future.

Proverbs 24:14 NCV

Your life is an adventure in decision-making . . . and the same thing can be said of your friendships. If you want to build strong, Christ-centered relationships, you must make wise decisions, and you must make them consistently.

Each day, all of us make countless decisions that hopefully bring us closer to God. When we obey God's commandments, we share in His abundance and His peace. But, when we turn our backs upon God by disobeying Him, we invite Old Man Trouble to stop by for an extended visit.

Do you want to be successful in life and in love? If so, here's a good place to start: Obey God. When you're faced with a difficult choice or a powerful temptation, pray about it. Invite God into your heart and live according to His commandments. When you do, you will be blessed today, and tomorrow, and forever.

The Reference Point for the Christian is the Bible.
All values, judgments, and attitudes must be gauged in
relationship to this Reference Point.

Ruth Bell Graham

Every day, I find countless opportunities to decide
whether I will obey God and demonstrate my love for Him
or try to please myself or the world system.
God is waiting for my choices.

Bill Bright

God always gives His best to those who leave
the choice with Him.

Jim Elliot

Remember This: First you'll make choices . . . and
before you know it, your choices will make you. So
choose carefully.

Your Best Friend Is Jesus: Walk with Him

Then he told them what they could expect for themselves:
"Anyone who intends to come with me has to let me lead."

Luke 9:23 MSG

Here's one last tip for you and your friends: behave yourselves like Christians every day of the week, not just on Sundays.

Jesus made an extreme sacrifice for you. Are you willing to make changes in your life for Him? Can you honestly say that you're passionate about your faith and that you're really following Jesus? Hopefully so. But if you're preoccupied with other things—or if you're strictly a one-day-a-week Christian—then you're in need of a big time spiritual makeover.

Jesus doesn't want you to be a run-of-the-mill, follow-the-crowd kind of believer. Jesus wants you to be a "new creation" through Him. And that's exactly what you should want for yourself, too.

So remember this: you're the recipient of Christ's love. Accept it enthusiastically and demonstrate your love with words and actions. Jesus deserves your heart—give it to Him today, tomorrow, and forever, Amen.

The dearest friend on earth is but a mere shadow compared with Jesus Christ.

Oswald Chambers

When we truly walk with God throughout our day, life slowly starts to fall into place.

Bill Hybels

Walk in the daylight of God's will because then you will be safe; you will not stumble.

Anne Graham Lotz

Remember This: If you want to follow in Christ's footsteps . . . welcome Him into your heart, obey His commandments, and share His never-ending love.